LUTON TOWN

THE NON-LEAGUE YEARS

LUTON TOWN

THE NON-LEAGUE YEARS

ROB HADGRAFT

AMBERLEY

'Cambridge have lost,' said the text on my phone. I read it twice, maybe three times and then screamed, 'We are champions!' I started to shake and could feel tears forming. I couldn't help screaming again and again.

Mary Scarlino, Luton Town fan, April 2014

People felt this club was wronged, I've helped right that wrong. That gives me a very, very special feeling. I'm proud to have given all those fans their dignity back. All of a sudden the sun's come out.

John Still, Luton Town manager, April 2014

First published 2014

Amberley Publishing
The Hill, Stroud
Gloucestershire, GL5 4EP

www.amberley-books.com

Copyright © Rob Hadgraft, 2014

The right of Rob Hadgraft to be identified as the Author
of this work has been asserted in accordance with the
Copyrights, Designs and Patents Act 1988.

British Library Cataloguing in Publication Data.
A catalogue record for this book is available from the British Library.

ISBN 978 1 4456 3893 5 (print)
ISBN 978 1 4456 3905 5 (ebook)

Typesetting and Origination by Amberley Publishing.
Printed in the UK.

Contents

Author's Note   6

Foreword   7

Prologue   9

1 2009/10 Season   15

2 2010/11 Season   47

3 2011/12 Season   72

4 2012/13 Season   96

5 2013/14 Season   115

Appendix   157

Author's Note

This book traces Luton Town's five highly eventful years in non-League football by way of month-by-month reportage, largely based on my observations from the nether regions of Block 'C', in front of the ancient Main Stand at Kenilworth Road. The views, opinions and memories are my own (unless quoted otherwise) and are founded on forty colourful years of watching the Hatters in five different divisions of the English football pyramid.

Supporting Luton can be a stressful business, and that seat in Block 'C' is not a comfortable one, but once you are hooked there's no turning back. I hope my narrative captures some of the sights, sounds and surreal flavours of a big club's temporary exile in the unforgiving, forbidding world outside the Football League. It was a strange and discomfiting five-year journey.

In getting the story of that journey published in book form, I called upon the help of the following, to whom I pass grateful thanks: LTFC chairman Nick Owen, Geoff Cox at the *Luton News*, my fellow bloggers Kevin Crowe (*Left Midfield*) and David Mosque (*For God's Sake What Now?*), not forgetting supporters Mary Scarlino, Roger Whichelow, Simon Darwen, Nick Pirie, Gavin Daly, Andrew Kingston and Josie Kingston. For picture credits, see individual captions.

Rob Hadgraft
July 2014

Foreword

Rob Hadgraft has previously written three forensically detailed epics on Luton Town FC, all of them focusing on some of the wretched events that have befallen the club in our often turbulent history since the late fifties. At last, what a relief! He's produced a book with a happy ending!

It tells the story of our five years in the Conference from the standpoint of a long-suffering fan (just like the rest of us!), and all the joys, despair, frustration and false dawns that brings. And, as we all know now, the non-League years ended in utter jubilation in April 2014, as we won the Skrill Premier title by a clear nineteen points with over 100 goals and more than 100 points. We broke records galore on the way.

So what has it been like, spending five years in exile from the Football League, dumped there by astonishingly harsh penalties? These were penalties that punished the innocent fans and the small but extraordinarily committed group of supporters, who actually rescued the club with their time or money or both when it was on the brink of extinction.

Well, for me – and I am sure there are tens of thousands who feel the same way – it has intensified my passion for Luton Town. I didn't ever believe I could care more than I did before, but somehow the way the authorities treated us in 2008, the searing sense of injustice, made it that much more imperative for me to see our beloved football club rise up and become successful again – to take our place once more among the game's elite.

I have thoroughly enjoyed individual moments during our five years away. I've watched some terrific games, visited loads of new grounds, made plenty of new friends and witnessed first-hand the rebirth of Luton Town, both on and off the field. As a club, we return to the Football League as a much leaner and considerably more robust outfit, with a clear strategy to make significant progress in the near future.

Our support has not only remained steadfast but has actually grown. The numbers who've turned up for home matches and followed us away are simply phenomenal. In the circumstances of what has happened in recent times, an outsider might think that is bizarre. Well, it isn't, because Luton fans, I reckon, are a breed apart, and there is something truly special about our club that makes it irresistible.

I am proud to be a Luton fan, and I know there are many thousands like me, both here and abroad. Thank goodness, as I write this in the early summer of 2014, we all feel on top of the world and we can enjoy Rob's take on the last five challenging years with, of course, a happy ending!

Nick Owen
Chairman, Luton Town FC
May 2014

Prologue

North London, 15 April 2014. It was 9.45 p.m. on a cool, clear Tuesday evening. Around 60,000 were dispersing from the Emirates Stadium, where Arsenal had just beaten West Ham in a game crucial to the race for Champions League places. In a street outside the ground, Mary Scarlino, a nursery nurse and mum who lives 37 miles away in the market town of Baldock, looked distracted and uncomfortable among the throng. Her mind was elsewhere. Her husband, a West Ham supporter, was anxious to get away from the scene of his team's defeat, but Mary was slowing him down.

She stopped walking and began struggling with a mobile phone, jabbing fingers impatiently at its keys, desperate to make it work after several hours with no signal. Suddenly, it sprang to life, and there was a text awaiting her. It was from her daughter Dannii back in Baldock. It was short and to the point: 'Cambridge have lost.' Mary stiffened, and for several moments didn't move a muscle as she took in the implications of this. Then she emitted a blood-curdling scream that startled the crowds making their way around her: 'Oh my God!' Mary supported neither Arsenal nor West Ham, her heart was beating for a team four divisions lower, a team not even playing that evening. Luton Town. And that simple message from her daughter had huge implications for Luton Town.

'I read that text twice,' Mary said, 'maybe three times and then screamed, WE ARE CHAMPIONS! I started to shake and could feel the tears forming. I couldn't help screaming again, and all these Arsenal and West Ham fans are staring at me wondering what is going on. Later on the train going home I'm still buzzing when an Arsenal fan leans over and says "Cambridge lost tonight, so Luton are Conference champions." All I can say back is "Yes we are!" with the biggest smile on my face you can imagine. When we finally got home I grabbed three glasses, one each for me, my hubby and daughter, and went straight to the fridge to finally open the champagne in there. After five years it had chilled nicely!'

Mary's champagne had been 'on ice' for five long years in readiness for the moment Luton Town escaped the dreaded Conference and could return to the Football League. She'd first placed it in the fridge in 2009 after a friend's wedding, but since then no fewer than four seasons had ended in disappointment, meaning it was left unopened. On 10 April 2014, it was put in an ice bucket, anticipating either a defeat for Luton's rivals Cambridge at Woking, or, failing that, a Luton win over Braintree two days later. Either of these outcomes would have seen Luton clinch the title, but both failed to materialise. Another three days passed before the wait was finally over.

Elsewhere, similar scenarios were being played out. Train driver Arthur Mason and his pal Brian had, in 2009, won a pub quiz at the Jolly Topers in Luton, their prize was a bottle of champagne. But with the Hatters having just been demoted that year, after stringent points deductions, the pair were in no mood to celebrate. They couldn't decide who should take the bottle home with them, so made a pact it would remain in the pub and only be opened the day Luton were promoted back to the League. Five long years later, their wait was over too. 'At 9.45 p.m. Brian and I met in the pub, bottle in hand, glasses ready. Five years on and God it tasted so, so good!' said Arthur.

Luton fan Mark Couch won his champagne in a competition just before the Johnstone's Paint Trophy final at Wembley in the spring of 2009. Luton beat Scunthorpe in a five-goal thriller, but Mark couldn't bring himself to celebrate because, a few days later, the team's relegation into non-League was confirmed. Mark told his mum he wouldn't open the bottle until the day the club returned to the League. Five years later, and his wait was also over, although his delight at Luton's success was tinged with sadness: 'My mum's sadly not with us any more to see it happen, but that bottle was emptied at about 11:30 p.m. Love you mum!'

Those were just three of thousands of scenarios played out across the globe on the evening of 15 April 2014. It wasn't just the sound of champagne corks popping either – there was an explosion of joy and relief that echoed for weeks afterwards. The celebrations were no less enthusiastic for the fact they were ignited on a night Luton didn't even play; the moment of truth was a 2-0 defeat at Kidderminster for Cambridge United, a result that mathematically ended the latter's slim chance of catching the Hatters at the top of English football's fifth tier.

That night thousands were pinned to radios, computers, tablets and cell phones, wondering if five years of miserable exile was about to be declared over. Of course, it was a shame the denouement wasn't in front of a packed and rocking Kenilworth Road ground, but at least emotions could be let loose via social media, where a remarkable faux party atmosphere was soon whipped up; Luton's big moment was trending on Twitter and goodness knows where else too. The scale of the jubilation was hardly surprising, for this was no ordinary promotion.

Football clubs bounce back from relegation on a reasonably regular basis, but this was well outside the norm. The perceived injustice of the way Luton departed the League in 2009, and the mounting frustration caused by four failures to return, had created a massive build-up of tension and emotion. No wonder the party would last for weeks.

Bizarrely, team manager John Still, the man who masterminded the outcome so many desperately wanted, heard the news himself from one of the four men Luton had ditched for failing to negotiate the road back from oblivion. It was Mick Harford – arguably the most popular employee in LTFC history – who spotted Still sitting nearby on scouting duty at Crawley Town, sidled over to him, gave him a playful bear hug and passed on the news Cambridge had lost and Luton were consequently champions. In typically laid-back style, Still had been concentrating on the game in front of him and not even monitoring events involving Cambridge.

Having received the headlines from Harford, Still's phone now sprang into life and didn't stop ringing for hours (the ringtone being 'Up the Junction' by Squeeze). First to offer congratulations was Brendan Rogers, boss of Premiership title-chasers Liverpool, whose message opened the floodgates. Still finally got to bed around 2 a.m. but was up again by 4 a.m., unable to sleep, his head buzzing with the implications of what had been achieved. Later that day, Still had a message for the jubilant fans:

> People have been getting a little edgy and desperate for this moment to come. Well it's now come, the moment has come, and you should go out and enjoy it because it doesn't happen often. I didn't have a drink last night, but will get legless tonight!

An astonishing list of ex-Luton players, managers, well-known football personalities, exiled fans and even the odd celebrity, posted on social media in the immediate aftermath of the Cambridge result. For example, Hollywood actor Colin Salmon stated, 'A genuinely great day for a great town.' BBC newsreader Faye Carruthers declared, 'Goosebumps! Such a proud Hatter. Thank you John Still, thank you.' England cricketer Monty Panesar whooped, 'Waited five years for this day – back to League football. Boom!' Club chairman and BBC news presenter Nick Owen confessed,

> I've been running around my living room celebrating, and just heard my daughter Jenny is doing exactly the same in Melbourne, Australia! We've won Wembley finals and been in the top league, but this perhaps tops the lot because we're coming back from so far down. A very special moment and I'm feeling very emotional.

He added that he'd just received a celebratory message from Eric Morecambe's son Gary.

Stage and television actor Simon Darwen said the chant 'Champions' began echoing around a London theatre production meeting when the result came through:

> I was in rehearsal for my biggest scene in the show *Catch 22*. I'd got twenty of the artiest and most non-footie people I know thinking about a match in Kidderminster! I had my phone in my pocket and when I saw the news I had to leave the stage and let out a blood-curdling swear word. My director – a New Yorker with no knowledge of soccer – sighed and casually ordered a tea break, saying 'It looks like Luton won the league then?'

One fan broadcast from an Indian restaurant that a fellow supporter had shocked diners by climbing up and dancing on tables when the news came through. And journalist Geoff Cox announced, 'I've seen fifteen promotions and relegations in fifty-three years of following my team and this is probably the sweetest moment yet.' Former Oxford, Rushden and Luton midfielder Andy Burgess said, 'I've won it as a player, now I've won it as a supporter.' Supporter Andy Aslam stated, 'And on the 15th day of April, the good Lord said let there be justice and the Hatters were finally set free.'

And so it went on. After five years out of the loop, Luton Town was big news again. Managing director Gary Sweet was hotly pursued for interviews, being uniquely qualified to summarise exactly how Luton had fallen from grace since 2006 to find themselves marooned in the Conference. Sweet had co-founded the consortium of lifelong fans who wrested control of the club after years of mismanagement. They turned things around despite massive sanctions from the authorities. Sweet oversaw club affairs throughout the five Conference years, the era described in detail in this book from my own viewpoint as a long-standing supporter.

According to him, demotion to the Conference always felt like being wrongly imprisoned, but now their time had been served and release was imminent. The good times were returning, even though it would be hard to completely erase all the bad memories:

> The lowest point was coming out of the League offices in July 2008 knowing we had a thirty-point deduction and were going to get relegated to the Conference the following May. It knocked the stuffing out of us. And this was shortly after we paid a few million to buy the club just as the global economy was entering recession.

Events on that awful day in 2008 centred on the League's London headquarters in Gloucester Place, where Sweet and the new owners were told that to get back their 'golden share' and continue as a League club they must accept a twenty-point deduction. This was in addition to an earlier ten-point penalty from the FA for admin offences. It meant Mick Harford and a squad assembled from scratch would start 2008/09 a massive thirty points adrift of the rest. It was an unprecedented and staggering hurdle to overcome and put the club's long history as a League club in serious jeopardy.

The severity was breathtaking and suggested the authorities had lost patience and were making an example of Luton to warn others not to live beyond their means. The twenty-point figure was said to have been imposed due to Luton being put in administration three times in less than ten years. In total, the authorities docked Luton forty points in less than nine months. The sting in the tail came when the club was told it could not appeal the decision. Waiving their right of appeal was part of the deal in getting the golden share back. If they didn't like it, the alternative was to quit the League straight away and start all over again in a minor league. It would be a fatal blow and Luton duly finished ninety-second in May 2009 and exited the League.

For a club that spent most of the 1980s in the top flight, reached two Wembley League Cup finals and three FA Cup semi-finals, it was a bitter pill to swallow, especially for us fans. As recently as the autumn of 2006, Luton were positioned near the top of the Championship, beating the likes of Crystal Palace, Leicester and Leeds. Just three years later, we found ourselves lining up against Kettering, Salisbury and Grays. To make matters worse, many fans wrongly assumed the club was far too strong to linger in non-League and would make a quick return. A huge fish in a tiny pool. But the Conference only allows one automatic promotion place per year and has become a tough league to get out of. As we now know, even a good season amassing eighty points or more doesn't guarantee success. The clubs in the Conference Premier are mostly fully professional and there is little difference in quality from League Two.

Even the most pessimistic Luton fan never expected it would take five years to escape. Having suffered the slings and arrows of outrageous Luton fortune on a regular basis since the mid-1970s, I always suspected it wouldn't be easy, but never anticipated five seasons and 238 matches in non-League circles (that figure includes eight play-off ties and two games declared null and void). Expectation levels remained sky-high throughout, as did attendances, but managers came and went as pressure and frustration mounted.

Those five years were laden with angst, frustration and occasional humiliation, but ultimately had a happy ending. There was plenty of well-documented moaning and groaning, but thankfully the loyal fan base kept the faith throughout. Who knows where we'd be now had attendances plummeted, leading to budget cuts and an inability to attract and recruit the right people? I lost count of the number of new players we signed who said a major factor in choosing Luton had been our big crowds.

It was a long and painful journey, but once John Still had harnessed the 'Team Luton' effect, we finally made it out. Writer and philosopher Leo Tolstoy, who knew a thing or two about lengthy struggles, wasn't wrong when he stated, 'The two most powerful warriors are patience and time.'

1

2009/10 Season

August 2009: 'Craddock, Has Your Dog Died?'

Luton Town were out of the big league after eighty-nine years, and we had to get used to the idea. This was not just a bad dream. The new reality bit immediately, for the first Blue Square Conference game was away from home, strictly an all-ticket affair, and in a trice our meagre allocation of 800 places was snapped up. Around twice that number of Luton fans were left disappointed.

Under an unforgiving August sun, the new English season of 2009/10 would get underway in a blaze of colour, goals and roaring crowds in famous old stadiums. But not for Luton Town. Our reality was having to muster in a field off the A2043 in Kingston-upon-Thames. We kicked off against AFC Wimbledon, in effect the humblest club playing at this level, having only existed since 2002. Welcome to the Conference.

If you think that was grim, our preseason tour won't have impressed you either – we pitched up at places like Ilfracombe, Appledore and Great Torrington, the footballing hotbeds of deepest Devon. The Errea South-West Challenge wasn't the most prestigious tournament available, but as a non-League club we now had to cut our cloth accordingly. It was clear summer jaunts to the USA and Asia would be off Luton's agenda for some time to come.

The one consolation in touring Devon instead of Dubai was its affordability. The loyal band of fans that can't bear to miss a single match, no matter how minor or inconsequential, could stalk their heroes without even leaving these shores. There were 250 of them, a figure that shocked the disbelieving locals. Perhaps inevitably, the whole escapade ended in mayhem, fellow tourists Grimsby Town throwing their toys out of the pram and refusing to play Luton – partly because of a row over kick-off times, and partly because their ex-Luton manager Mike Newell was sick of all the 'banter' coming his way from Luton's unforgiving travelling army.

The Devon farce was soon forgotten when Manchester United, no less, sent a team to Luton for a preseason warm-up. A crowd of 7,468 rolled up on a balmy evening, astonishing for a meaningless friendly against Fergie's youth team. Manager Mick Harford had by now assembled a decent-looking squad for the non-League sabbatical, which we all believed would be a mercifully brief and possibly even an interesting little interlude among football's poor relations. Sadly, this positive spin would fail to sustain itself for long.

When the friendlies were over, the serious business got underway at Wimbledon's Kingsmeadow home. We quite enjoyed the novelty of it all: marvelling at the bacon cheeseburgers 'specially for away fans', which were £4 a pop, joining in the minute's applause for the late Sir Bobby Robson, and welcoming the big reception from home fans for our manager Harford. Best of all, we cheered heartily when an over-enthusiastic Womble mascot had his head knocked off and was then thrown out of the ground by stewards – apparently for provoking Luton fans. The furry freak's goading was an unwise move that saw his wheelie bin and false head toppled spectacularly. The game itself ended all-square, both goals from the spot. Luton debutant Shane Blackett was sent off for an innocuous-looking challenge. Refereeing standards are lower in this league, we'd been warned, and when large crowds are involved, officials can be easily influenced by the unfamiliar pressures.

Three nights later, a semblance of normality at home was regained when we locked horns with the Stags of Mansfield – a team who had only recently arrived in the Conference after seventy-seven years as a League club. Luton versus Mansfield in front of 7,000-plus doesn't feel like non-League at all. A mystery man occupied our left-back slot – last-minute signings were rare in the League, so was this how things worked down here? Turns out he was Irishman Freddie Murray, a former Blackburn man on loan from Grays Athletic. Bizarre really, because Murray only joined Grays a week earlier, along with eight others, but a sudden change of management led him to cut his losses and join us hours before kick-off. It's a madhouse in the Conference – get used to it folks!

On another balmy evening perfect for football, we gave the Stags a 4-1 tonking, coming back from a goal behind. Centre-back George Pilkington netted a brace, and when we won a penalty it looked like history in the making – a hat-trick by a centre-half – until the ball was wrestled away from him by Claude Gnakpa. Then the Frenchman was also deemed unsuitable for penalty duties, and further wrestling saw the proper penalty-taker, Tom Craddock, win the day.

Four points so far meant we soared to second in the table, FA points deductions meaning we were twenty-nine points ahead of poor old Chester City. There was no crowing about that, because nobody knows better than us what a points deduction feels like. A few days later, Gateshead were in town, a club we hadn't played in ninety years – and even then they had a different name (South Shields). Fresh out of the Conference North, with gates of a few hundred, they are the smallest club to visit Kenilworth Road for a league fixture in ninety years or more. The Oak Road away section was quiet and underpopulated, housing just forty-six fans. Something else we needed to get used to.

Luton looked nervous and unsettled, and there was huge relief when Asa Hall and Kevin Gallen scored within a minute of each other to set up victory. The consensus that we shouldn't be in this league at all led to the belief we ought to look a class above this sort of opposition. But on this day we didn't. A crowd of nearly 7,000 was underwhelmed by what they witnessed. Boos and catcalls at the end; we'd hit the top of the table, but many fans were distinctly unhappy.

The level of expectation here was now crystal clear. Top of the pile, yet still the fans were grumbling. Manager Harford must have loved that little paradox. Especially as the next game was a trip to Forest Green Rovers, a banana skin if there ever was one. I was reminded of the well-worn story about the radio reporter at a Raith Rovers game who used the line, 'They'll be dancing in the streets of Raith tonight,' blissfully unaware Raith is not actually a place at all. Well, that's also the case with Forest Green. Luton fans were warned not to bother looking under 'F' when consulting road atlases. FGR's little stadium is just outside the small town of Nailsworth, and sits atop a hill, amid fields of sheep, deep in the Cotswolds. And when the sun goes down, it gets exceedingly chilly up there.

Luton fans marvelled at the FGR chairman greeting the crowd individually at the main gate. Others reported having seen a field of llamas on the drive in. We parked at the local primary school in an area that looked as if Compo and Clegg from *Last of the Summer Wine* would go cycling by at any moment. The surprisingly impressive Main Stand featured a bar specialising in local ales, with chips and curry sauce on the menu. Around half the crowd of just under 2,000 were from Luton. We made enough noise to keep the sheep and llamas awake, but sadly our team served up some stodgy fare again. Harford's tactics came under fire. He started with three at the back and five in midfield, but after an awful first half, he changed things around – to little effect. As darkness cloaked the Cotswolds, Craddock netted the game's only goal with a neat piece of poaching, and not long afterwards thumped a penalty against the bar. That excitement apart, this was a real stinker. To win when you play poorly is of course a great habit, but we surely wouldn't keep this up for much longer?

Crisis-club Chester were next, playing catch-up after a delayed start to the season. It seemed their hard-core fans had given up on the current rabble and were waiting for things to go completely pear-shaped, so they could band together and create a brand new club from the ashes – just like Aldershot Town and AFC Wimbledon did. There were only eighty-five visiting fans sitting forlornly at the Oak Road end, but they got a nice surprise when title favourites Luton failed to brush their makeshift outfit aside. We had skipper Kevin Nicholls back from suspension, but again failed to click. Can this really have been the same team that won so thrillingly at Wembley just months ago? On paper this should have been no contest, but Chester went closest, hitting the bar as Luton passes went astray and flowing football was again absent. Ninety grim minutes went by and the two sides relegated from the Football League failed to trouble the scorers. Jeers rang out and Harford looked crestfallen as he trooped down the tunnel.

Despite being unbeaten after five games, Luton had been booed off by their own fans three games in a row. A popular theory was that teams playing Luton treated it as their 'cup final' and consequently raised their game due to the bigger crowds and better atmosphere. They were certainly stifling us and preventing the goal-fests we naively expected. At least crowds were holding up well, and some old fans were even returning to the fold. Eric Morecambe's son Gary, for example, started attending again, following in the footsteps of another celebrity fan – performance poet John Hegley. The latter was a devoted boyhood supporter who fell out of the habit, but saw the error of his ways in Luton's hour of need.

A new experience for the seasoned fans was a local derby with Kettering, and a big turnout of nearly 2,000 Hatters fans made the short trip into Northants. The size of the invasion prompted local police to bring out horses and helicopters, which seemed an overreaction. The Poppies' modest old stadium was not the most picturesque or comfortable, especially the wonky away end. To rub salt into our wounds, a Kettering director referred to our esteemed chairman as 'Nick Ross, TV personality from *Crimewatch*' in the matchday programme. Nick Owen is a personable chap and no doubt resisted the temptation to put the record straight in the boardroom afterwards.

We suspected Luton performances were slowly getting worse – and the trend was confirmed at Kettering in a goalless bore. Mark Tyler made a couple of sharp saves but generally it was a bad, bad game. Black humour abounded: one fan shouted that Craddock was moping around as if his dog had died. Somebody else told us seven successive Luton 'attacks' had involved a long ball from the back falling straight to an unchallenged opponent. The game was so drab that radio reporters amused themselves discussing the military aircraft passing overhead and the strange plastic owl that sits above the press box at Rockingham Road. At the end, skipper Nicholls acknowledged the huge away support in time-honoured fashion, but was cut short by cries of 'rubbish' and worse. Looking surprised, he responded with shrugging gestures that could have been either an apology, or him asking why we were so unhappy at having won a point. Depressing stuff either way.

September 2009:
The Cheeky Kid from Down the Road

I always thought George Edward Pilkington sounded more like a character from a Brontë novel than a twenty-eight-year-old rock at the heart of Luton's defence. Blue Square Player of the Month, he became our unlikely leading scorer by netting twice at home to Crawley. After 249 minutes without a goal to cheer, the sheer relief sparked an unusual event, Pilks leading the team to the dugouts where they mobbed manager Harford – a surprise gesture of solidarity after all the negative stuff he'd suffered recently. Craddock swooped to make it a comfortable 3-0, and we were in cruise control.

Next up was a trip to the prosaically named Raymond McEnhill Stadium. It's the home of Salisbury City, just across the road from historic Old Sarum hill fort, a former rotten borough now run by English Heritage. Most visitors to these parts are students, professors of history and mystics – football fans are in the minority. One of the Luton coaches nearly drove straight past, simply because it just didn't look like a football ground from outside. As with Chester, Salisbury had our sympathy; 48 hours earlier they'd announced they were going into administration, a move that instantly erased the hard-earned ten points they'd won so far this season. With the princely total of zero points, they sank to twenty-third in the table – but still ahead of Chester (minus twenty-four).

Although Luton fans numbered almost 1,000 (higher than Salisbury's entire home gate for a recent match), all noise disappeared upwards into the vast Wiltshire sky and the whole occasion felt a bit flat. Our well-travelled forward Kevin Gallen stretched his ageing limbs to poke in the opening goal, but prolific Matt Tubbs (not as fat as he sounds) pulled the home side level. All manner of huffing and puffing failed to yield a winner. Four wins and four draws from eight games thus far for Luton, and Oxford were starting to pull away at the top. They seemed to have finally got the measure of this league in their fourth season down here. Surely it wouldn't take Luton that long?

A chance to peg them back came three days later. Harford's barmy army found itself snarled up in horrendous traffic around the Kassam Stadium in Oxford. Out here on the edge of the city, there was no sign of the famous dreaming spires, nor dons on bicycles, for we were in the vicinity of the infamous trouble spot, the Blackbird Leys housing estate. It was well-known for joyriding and dangerous car stunts, although there was little chance of anyone speeding this night, such was the congestion caused by the match. Luton fans clicked the turnstiles no fewer than 2,331 times, astonishing for a midweek BSP league game that was 70 miles from home. It's an away following rarely exceeded by some Premiership clubs. The ground was packed to the gills with 10,613 – a record since the Conference was rebranded in 2007. The atmosphere was red hot in a 'proper' football ground, the occasion reminiscent of our Championship days of less than five years ago. Everyone in the Luton section was wide-eyed, noisy and very much up for it, but within minutes of kick-off we were deflated and 2-0 behind. There had been a terrific roar from the Luton section when Tyler saved highly rated Constable's penalty, but the ball was immediately regained by Oxford to create another opening Constable didn't miss; it was high to low in less than 40 seconds. Shortly afterwards, a shot by Cook flew into the net to bring a sick feeling to the pit of every Luton stomach.

There were signs of trouble breaking out as the unhappy atmosphere intensified. Realistic hopes of a comeback disappeared early in the second period when Nicholls executed one of his rashest challenges in a career littered with rash challenges – it was high, dangerous and ridiculously late. Nicholls, not as sharp as he once was, got there as soon as he could – it was a clear red card. At 2-0 down, our hopes of a comeback departed with him and there was no further scoring.

After nine games, Luton were now fourth. This was not what the 2020 management team and the fans envisaged. What were previously just moans and groans escalated into calls for Harford's head, and Nicholls' place in the team, let alone his captaincy, was questioned. It was hard to believe a manager would be sacked after one defeat in nine games, but at Luton there were extraordinary expectation levels. We were in the fifth tier due to points penalties, not because we were a poor team – so an instant return to level four was demanded. But Harford had had little luck and was hampered by injuries and suspensions.

Our next visitors Barrow disappeared from the League in 1972 (replaced by Hereford), rarely to be heard of again. They featured in one of the very first matches I ever saw as an impressionable ten-year-old, and I recall marvelling at their strange name, their stout goalkeeper Fred Else, and the fact they came from even further north than the Lake District. But they were not pleasing to behold in 2009, packing midfield and defence and frustrating the hell out of us. The day's only goal came when winger Adam Newton's cross looped apologetically into the Barrow net. Clearly an honest sort, Newton refused to celebrate, acknowledging it was a fluke. Our only real fun came from jeering Deasy, one of the noisiest, bulkiest goalkeepers to have visited in recent years. Every save was followed by his clambering furiously to his feet to berate a colleague. At one point, he even got angry with his own boots and held the game up to change them. The more the crowd cheered at his discomfort, the angrier he got.

A few days later, the game at home to York was called off. Bedfordshire constabulary was reportedly fully occupied that day, having had to prevent an illegal demonstration from taking place elsewhere in town. Basically, the game was called off because of a demonstration that wasn't happening – weird or what? Would the same thing have occurred for a Football League game? It created a ten-day gap between games, which meant Harford had plenty of time to plan an assault on North Wales to face Dean Saunders' Wrexham. No trouble finding this one – it's easy to spot the Racecourse Ground as you swing off the A483. It's a stadium occasionally used for Welsh internationals, a proper football ground with big, red crush barriers, terracing and traditional floodlight pylons. More than 300 hardy Hatters made the long round trip, blissfully unaware they were about to see 'history' in the making.

After witnessing a contest that plumbed the depths, Harford declared unequivocally this must be the worst display in Luton's entire history. Quite a claim in view of some of those capitulations in the mid-sixties! Harford isn't a man who says things just to grab a headline or two – he was genuinely shaken by what he'd witnessed. With both Nicholls and Keith Keane missing, we were a soft touch, no bite in midfield and some players looking like they'd rather be anywhere else than North Wales on this Tuesday night. The home side netted three of thirteen attempts, we bagged zero from two. The new table showed us down to ninth. In the great scheme of things, we were now ranked 101st in England – the lowest point in my lifetime and quite probably in the last 100 years or so. No wonder Harford said what he said. Having fallen through that dreaded trapdoor in April, four months later it felt like we were still fumbling around in the dark and struggling to find our feet.

After the game, the manager said a 'heart to heart' had taken place, but admitted even that was a failure. The players didn't take the chance to thrash things out between them and left him to 'do the nailing', as he put it. The fallout back in Bedfordshire after this debacle was immense, particularly via social media and suchlike. The general feeling was that Harford, however much loved and respected for previous achievements, had to go. One or two allegations were made that Luton players were seen 'looking cheerful' during the post-match warm down, which, if true, was highly disrespectful towards fans who had travelled hundreds of miles. The club refuted this and a feud developed involving the local BBC radio station. Particularly inflammatory was a rumour the players enjoyed a horse racing outing shortly after the dreadful display at Wrexham. It was never made clear if this had been a private outing organised among themselves, or an official team-bonding exercise. Whatever the truth, it went down badly with the paying public.

The opportunity to put things right came at Cambridge United, another former League outfit suffering hard times. Jogging across Coldham's common to get to the ground, I fell in line with the gaggle of Luton fans being scrutinised by Cambridgeshire police, snarling Alsatians straining at the leash, and helicopters overhead. Despite the poor fare recently being served on the field, more than 1,700 Hatters fans turned out. We packed the Habbin Terrace and South Stand and made one hell of a racket. This was going to be a good day – you could feel it in the air.

But things started badly, and then went from bad to worse. Ex-Hatter Pitt netted for the home side, a disputed penalty doubled that lead, and to cap it all we lost striker Liam Hatch to an avoidable red card. It looked grim. Several disillusioned Luton fans could take no more and left at half-time. But after thirty-five years of following Luton I know this is all part of the white-knuckle ride; bailing out before the end is not an option. The only time I ever left early was to avoid missiles during the Millwall riots of 1985. My view is that walking out early is all very well as a gesture of disgust, but think how sick you'd feel to miss a dramatic comeback. I must be a 'glass half-full' person.

And yes, miracles do happen. We may have been 0-2 behind with ten men, but Luton found the wherewithal to reward us with 45 minutes that will live long in the memory. Harford must have given one hell of a team talk at the break, for we were a side transformed. Gallen pulled a goal back, hoisting noise levels upwards again. He resembled a man on a mission, screaming for the volume to go yet higher, fists clenched, face contorted and arms waving. It was good to see a former top-flight player so committed to the cause at non-League level. This is what we needed. Before long, Rossi Jarvis combined neatly with rampant Gallen to score an absolute peach of an equaliser. The away stands were rocking and, remarkably, ten-man Luton looked the only likely winners. Local lad Jake Howells nipped in for his career-first goal to put us 3-2 ahead, and amid the mayhem that followed, he overdid the celebrating and collapsed injured. Cambridge then bounced back with an equaliser, but Gallen won it 4-3 from the spot to spark celebrations as if we'd won the title. Murray – a former Cambridge player – even donated his shirt to the heaving throng. The mad frenzy to get hold of this souvenir reflected the fact the club shop hadn't taken delivery of replica shirts yet.

Harford was suddenly off the hook, so maybe that outing to the races wasn't such a bad idea after all? The biggest crowd in nearly two years (8,223) assembled at Kenilworth Road three days later for our first serious local derby with Stevenage. I have to confess to a long-held prejudice that that night's opponents are a horrendous bunch – direct, physical and keen on gamesmanship, crimes that we Luton purists abhor! Their manager Graham Westley even founded a consulting business called AIMITA (an acronym for 'Attitude Is More Important Than Ability'). I rest my case.

Westley's mob looked strong, well organised and pumped up by the atmosphere. Crowds of 8,000 at this level are almost unheard of, so his motivational mumbo-jumbo wasn't even needed. The game proved a tense, intriguing struggle as the clock ticked relentlessly on with the score sheet blank. Goalkeeper Chris Day (whose day job was landlord of The Crooked Billet) made one brilliant save, but generally Luton were held at bay. It began to dawn that we were not going to beat these 'nuisance neighbours', no matter how hard we toiled. The anti-Harford brigade's dander was up, and in the Main Stand some barrackers were also having a dig at the board.

It was a dose of harsh reality that was hard to swallow – could we really be struggling to score against little Stevenage at Kenilworth Road? A club with our history and resources? As we gloomily mulled this over, the unthinkable happened: with the final whistle looming, visiting left-back Laird raced into acres of space to crack home a fine winner. Right in front of 793 Stevenage fans, who went berserk. An awful silence fell on other parts of the ground. People held their head in their hands. Goalless would have been bad enough, but now we'd been mugged by the cheeky kid from down the road. Luton players trooped off stony faced as Stevenage's celebrated manically. Harford fronted up bravely by not disappearing quickly down the tunnel. However, his posture was more stooped than usual, his face drawn and full of torment. Body language speaks a thousand words. He gazed tight-lipped up into the Main Stand as boos and jeers filled the night air. The tunnel at Luton is positioned in the noisiest and most reactionary corner of the ground. There's no hiding place on a night like this, and to Harford it must have felt like the most uncomfortable place in the world.

He later spelled things out to BBC radio: 'Luton Town should be beating Stevenage with the players we have available.' The subdued interview ended with Harford being asked if he would resign, a question few Luton fans ever thought they would hear. After a short, dramatic pause came the reply, 'No, come on, be serious.'

After thirteen games this season, there had only been occasional glimpses of good, purposeful football. The opposition, without exception, had always been 'up for it', better organised and more resolute than expected. The second half at Cambridge was the only sustained period to live up to our demanding expectations. The opening two months of non-League life had felt like one big struggle, and we were adrift of leaders Oxford by thirteen points. One fan summed it up: 'The games are really not enjoyable – we seem to be having more fun in the pubs before the games than during the 90 minutes itself. It never used to be like that.'

October 2009: Spicy Soup at Aggborough

The big man had gone. The dastardly deed was done after dark, during a meeting at the ground. Mick Harford, a legend among fans young and old and currently working his fifth stint at Kenilworth Road, was shown the door. Mutual consent, they ere saying, but we all knew that's just a boring euphemism. Rarely can a dismissal have been so reluctantly carried out. There was much talk of heavy hearts, anguish and respect.

The axe fell twenty-four hours after those ugly scenes against Stevenage – although we were assured plans were underway to make changes even before that defeat. Harford was at the helm for twenty-one months, just about the most turbulent period in Hatters history. He oversaw two relegations, the exit from the League and a Wembley cup win. His ninety-one games in charge produced twenty-five victories, but even his harshest critics will appreciate the huge difficulties he inherited. The sympathy and good wishes washing around was not hypocritical hogwash – it all seemed genuinely felt. Coach Alan Neilson, a likeable, enthusiastic sort, was given caretaker charge while managers with non-League experience such as Gary Brabin, Paul Tisdale and Mark Cooper were touted as favourites to take over permanently. Wycombe sacked Peter Taylor days after Harford left, meaning he was immediately linked with Luton.

The dawning of a post-Harford era focused a few minds, and the team got stuck into Tamworth at Kenilworth Road. Asa Hall and debutant Ben Wright netted fine goals and we were on our way. A blustery wind prevented flowing football and the visitors pulled one back, but we hung in there.

Off to the home of Kidderminster Harriers, once managed by pie-munching Jan Molby, to face a club immensely proud of its home cooking. The spicy Aggborough soup, cottage pie and other goodies were of an unusually high calibre. For a football ground, that is. There was no false modesty here either, Kidderminster having erected a big sign proclaiming 'The best food in football'. Against the run of play, Barnes-Homer punished an error to put us behind. Some feisty challenges sparked the atmosphere into life, and Jarvis – often criticised for being too lightweight – was red-carded for a high challenge. Home forward Matthews then placed his boot dangerously near Tyler's face as the 'keeper saved, and another red card was brandished. The chant 'Sunday League referee' was soon being bellowed at the harassed official.

We were kept fretting until 75 minutes, but it was worth the wait, Newton thumping a wonderful equaliser on the volley. It crashed in via the underside of the bar, which made it look even better. In the dying seconds, all our pressure, and the raucous support from behind the goal, was rewarded when sub Ryan Charles swooped on a cross to net a superb winner. Harford was said to be popular with his players, and the same goes for caretaker Neilson. Skipper Nicholls took matters into his own hands after the game by going public with a plea that Neilson be given the job permanently. As a show of unity this was fine, but it could be seen as undermining the board, who were interviewing external candidates.

Neilson advanced his own case further by overseeing a third successive win, at Altrincham, which raised us to fifth in the table. Craddock silenced the posher part of Manchester by netting a penalty winner, with Tyler already having saved one at the other end. It was a good day out for Luton fans, a far cry from the days of intellectual Thomas de Quincey, whose seminal work *Confessions of an English Opium Eater* suggested Altrincham was best observed through the haze of an artificial stimulant. Opium was his choice, whereas the Hatters army evidently preferred a frothy glass of Boddingtons.

There was still no sign of a new manager and a flu virus was attacking the club when York came to town. It was no classic, and York scored first, so when burly Alan White somehow managed to burst the ball, it provided welcome light relief. Hall equalised and it ended all square, a big talking point being the poor form of skipper Nicholls. Did he have the flu too, was his chronic knee problem playing up, or was this Luton legend simply past his best? A week later, Neilson took the opportunity to do a bit of fashionable 'rotation' when Grays arrived for an FA Cup qualifying round tie – a stage of the competition not requiring Luton's participation in the past. Fans gave it the thumbs down, less than a third of the normal league gate turning up for a routine 3-0 win.

On the last Friday of the month came the announcement of the new manager. By lunchtime, amid crashing computers and delays at the club, it leaked out unofficially that our man was Richard Money, former Walsall and Scunthorpe manager, who played for us during the golden David Pleat era of the early 1980s. His former admirers at Walsall told us we had got a good one here, and passed on the important information that his nickname up there was Dickie Dosh!

Money's lack of experience at non-League level was covered by the fact Gary Brabin, last year's Conference Manager of the Year with Cambridge, also joined the management team. But those expecting a raucous welcoming ceremony were disappointed at the home game with Rushden & Diamonds the next day. Money strolled quietly out, the whole thing feeling distinctly low-key, and the applause was so muted it almost seemed his appointment was not universally popular. Perhaps folk simply didn't recognise him, for as a player he had a fine head of dark hair, but was now as bald as a billiard ball. It was a modest, business-like greeting, for he was clearly not a man for badge-kissing, fist-clenching or scarf-waving histrionics.

With Money looking on, Luton worked frantically to impress. Craddock had two first-half goals disallowed and hit a post. Rushden looked ordinary but well drilled in the low arts of time-wasting and causing frustration. They started running down the clock in the first half, and the referee finally took action against this on 55 minutes. Stifling Luton and annoying our crowd worked a treat, for we looked hapless late on and they duly pinched two goals. Mugged again right at the death. The jeers rang out and all this tension and frustration was remarkable considering it was only October. If Richard Money had underestimated the pressure and expectation levels here at Luton, he had been quickly put right.

November 2009: Like a Parachute in Reverse

Football League opposition in an FA Cup tie and it felt like normality had returned to Kenilworth Road. But as we were the humble non-League underdogs, we had to respectfully tip hats and bend knees to visiting League Two 'giants' Rochdale. Luckily our forgotten man, Steve Basham, was in no mood to bow and scrape, and bagged two goals in the first half hour, adding to one from Newton. Radical changes by Money seemed to be working. As well as Basham's call-up, the manager dropped feisty skipper Nicholls. The official line involved talk of a troublesome hip and sore knees. It was a statement that gave more credence to the cheeky terrace banter about our hero's dwindling shelf life.

Rochdale, in strange purple kit, surged back into the tie, scoring thrice to force a replay. Talk about a game of two halves. Our new manager looked baffled and unhappy to hear a few boos at the end. He would have to learn that Luton fans often booed an outcome, not necessarily the team's efforts. He duly had a pop at what he called 'negativity surrounding Kenilworth Road'. Surely he could appreciate this frustration among fans who had seen their club crowbarred out of the League just three years after enjoying Championship football?

The Rochdale replay was live on ITV, but 129 from Luton still preferred to witness the action in the flesh. Rochdale was cold, damp, but interesting in a bleak sort of way: it is the birthplace of the Co-op, and there was also Arif's Cash & Carry, the Ratcliffe Arms near the ground, mushy peas with your chips, dark satanic mills and Saddleworth Moor glowering on the horizon. Not forgetting draughty old Spotland, a lower division ground of limited charm since 1921.

Those who stayed behind and watched from their sofa enjoyed a surreal moment when hearing 'Hatters, Hatters, what a great team' coming over loud and clear via the ITV coverage. It was rare exposure for a thirty-five-year-old song recorded by ancient Bedfordshire-based chart-toppers The Barron Knights.

Our opponents were playing their thirty-fifth successive year in football's fourth tier. The last time they played a league game in another division was in April 1974 – the same day Luton clinched promotion to the top flight. Since then, we have enjoyed eleven seasons in the top tier, seventeen at the second level, plus a handful of trips to Wembley. For all our misery, perhaps we should have been grateful life was at least varied here at Luton.

After each side hit the woodwork, Craddock's cross was flicked expertly home by Gallen – a goal out of the blue. 'Cometh the hour, cometh the man!' screamed the commentator. Gallen was a wily old fox and this came fifteen years after his first strike in this competition. Near the end, he converted another and we were through. The reward was Rotherham away in round two, but at least we'd beaten what the television boys felt was Rochdale's best-ever team. Gracie Fields, Cyril Smith, Lisa Stansfield, Don Estelle, Andy Kershaw, Bill Oddie: your boys took a hell of a beating!

Next, we tackled a trip to the greyness that is Grays, complete with brand new goalkeeper, the reassuringly large Kevin Pilkington. The former Manchester United custodian must have been thinking he'd stepped onto the set of an Ingmar Bergman film, for the Essex backwater of Grays in the pouring rain was beyond bleak. It made even Rochdale feel homely. A steady stream of cars containing Luton fans arrived in the quiet town centre, seemingly the only traffic around. As they spilled their handsome contents – orange shirts lighting up the surroundings – some announced they'd heard on the radio that a pitch inspection was planned. Others were convinced the game was already off, while the rest just looked glum and dived back inside their cars to wait for the rain to ease.

Once upon a time, you only had to look for floodlight pylons to find a football ground in a strange town – not the case these days, especially in the Conference. Pylons are not what they used to be: smaller, lightweight constructions and not visible from far away. Grays' home was tricky to locate, the best clue being the cluster of dubious characters checking passing fans for tickets and weaponry. They told us they were stewards on loan from Leyton Orient. It was a modern and unusual little stadium; after the players warmed up they mysteriously disappeared into the ground floor of a block of flats. 'The toilets are excellent, the best part of the ground!' piped up one discerning Luton fan. In the programme editorial, the Grays club secretary rather bafflingly passed on information about his cats Honey and Treacle and his dog Bex.

The on-loan stewards took pity on us due to the horrendous weather and allowed umbrellas into the ground. Just before kick-off, a huge cheer went up when one brolly skittered in the wind, upwards and out of the ground towards Tilbury docks, rather like a parachute in reverse. A stout, middle-aged resident of the adjacent block of flats suddenly appeared on his balcony and settled down to watch the game, seemingly undaunted by the rain. He got a cheer from nearby Luton fans, but failed to see the funny side. The poor fellow looked increasingly uncomfortable as the songs began, accusing him of not buying a ticket and other misdemeanours.

The churning wind took the ball all over the shop. One corner swirled almost out of the ground. Conditions like these can be a great leveller, but under Money we were beginning to look organised and businesslike. Craddock and Gallen scored either side of the break, and the home side accepted defeat with wry inevitability. When the PA announcer read out the Man of the Match winner (a home player, in time-honoured fashion), the Luton fans let out a huge cry of 'Who?' to which he responded by reading it again. A second 'Who?' prompted a third reading, by which time everyone was in fits.

Runaway leaders Oxford lost at Kidderminster, so we had now closed the gap to six points and were fourth. It does seem that since Harford had left the helm, the ship was slowly making headway. Two days later, Sky Sports allowed us to wallow in nostalgia by screening an edition of *Time of Our Lives* starring Luton legends of the glorious 1980s, Ricky Hill, Brian Stein and Steve Foster. Another reminder, if we needed one, of how times change.

Before kick-off at the visit of Cambridge United, I spotted John Hegley, renowned performance poet and Luton fan, heading into the ground. He looked thoughtful and I suspected he must be in the process of composing a new ode about life in the Conference. A wonder goal by Craddock and a Gnakpa volley gave us a healthy 2-0 lead, but Cambridge were thrown a lifeline through another blunder by Nicholls, whose loose pass was turned in by Crow. Moments later, we celebrated home debutant Pilkington saving a penalty, but soon after this Nicholls sent Crow flying into the air for a second attempt. This time there was no mistake and it ended 2-2. The only consolation was the game being a fine advert for Conference football, and probably better fare than any of our twenty-three home games of last season in League Two.

'Dickie Dosh' then engineered a flurry of transfer activity, bringing in Matthew Barnes-Homer from Kidderminster, Coventry winger Ashley Cain, and sending three out on loan. A highly unconventional league ground was our next destination; FA Cup opponents Rotherham were hosting their small but noisy army of fans at Sheffield's international athletics arena, the Don Valley Stadium. We played second fiddle for long periods but fast-raiding Gnakpa won a penalty and Craddock put us ahead. We then conceded twice before diminutive sub Mark Nwokeji finished with a deft dink to ensure a replay. Equally impressive was the elaborate bow in his celebration routine.

Our new manager was by now proving good value, if rather baffling, in his interviews. He condemned those fans questioning his signing of Barnes-Homer for £75,000, saying, 'My feelings on this are summed up by two words – imagination and jealousy.' Puzzling but entertaining stuff.

December 2009:
Paralysing Abuse, Poisonous Atmosphere

Big, bad Kettering seemed to be playing with a new freedom after the departure of pragmatic manager Mark Cooper, and looked as good as any Conference side we'd seen thus far. They proved tough to break down at Kenilworth Road and our anxiety levels soared. The blind faith that a Luton winner would eventually come evaporated after the hour mark when Partridge curled a fine goal into our top corner. At least Davis and Roper, the two ex-Hatters in their team, had the good grace not to join the celebrations.

We were attacking our favourite end, but the expected late rally simply failed to materialise. Where had the fight gone? This was unacceptable stuff. We seemed unable to rise to the occasion at home these days, especially when teams tried to spoil and subdue. With the exception of the battling Keane, the team and staff were jeered off to loud chants of 'What a load of rubbish'. The manager made a show of enthusiastically applauding all four sides of the ground. Was that defiance? Irony? Who can tell.

Money later sounded exasperated, reflecting on a 'doom and gloom' mentality at the club, and unrealistic levels of expectation: 'We won't overreact and lose our heads while others around us are losing theirs,' he said through tight lips. Was he right? Were we losing our heads? We were by now sixteen points behind Oxford and down in eighth place, a thoroughly depressing scenario. The halfway point of the season was nearly reached, and the club was at an all-time low. Fellow fan James Garley spoke for many of us:

> We have absolutely no chance of winning this league now. Can it get any worse? Walking back to the car in the bitter cold and swirling rain after a home defeat to Kettering. How much more can we be expected to take?

Meanwhile, next opponents Chester, despite non-payment of debts and other misdemeanours, had survived expulsion from the Conference, at least for the time being. They had occupied Deva Stadium in Bumpers Lane since 1992, but their penury meant the place was already looking neglected.

Luton fans were channelled into the APC Overnight Stand. We hoped that name wouldn't mean we'd be kept there all night – the 90-minute stay was to prove more than enough. Although Chester were forced to field a makeshift side, the contest ended goalless. We seized on moments of light relief to stay awake – such as the PA announcer chuntering on about rain being on the way, meaning the owner of a Saab parked outside the ground might like to go and put his roof down.

When Barnes-Homer was fouled, a clear penalty was denied but the referee sent off the home defender, thus managing to infuriate both teams in one fell swoop. It summed the day up. Several hundred Luton fans unleashed verbal venom at their own team long before the end. Some of it was understandable, but some over the top. The manager and the off-form Murray and Barnes-Homer took the brunt. Money would later state, 'I have never before been subjected to the abuse I received at Chester. I remember walking off the pitch thinking – wow, what is going on here?'

Constant barracking can paralyse young players, and a negative, poisonous atmosphere definitely affects performance. All this was becoming obvious to our opponents, who now realised the way to tackle Luton was to spoil and frustrate as much as possible so that Hatters' fans turned on their own team. Strangely, amid all this turmoil we seemed to cope with a higher class of opposition far better than with the small fry. Not only did we turn Rotherham over 3-0 in the FA Cup replay, there was the sublime sound of Luton fans crying 'ole' as we passed our way around our crestfallen visitors. Fickle? You bet. Exactly fifty years after reaching the FA Cup final at Wembley we were now set to become the last surviving non-League club in this year's competition. Nicholls had his best game in ages, supplying Newton for a well-taken opener, and then flighting a free-kick for White's diving header to put us two up before half-time. Gnakpa slotted a fine third, and his celebrations proved highly entertaining, flapping his arms manically to urge noise levels even higher.

But just as we seemed to have found a bit of form, we had to field a team in the low-priority FA Trophy where we were 3-0 down within 40 minutes at Cambridge United. It led to an unprecedented number of Luton fans leaving the ground before half-time, presumably headed for the city centre pubs. A major reshuffle took place and performance improved, but we only pulled one back. During the latter half of the month, heavy snow blanketed large swathes of the UK, causing postponement of games with Forest Green and Histon and meaning that Christmas 2009 came and went with Luton outside the top six and fourteen points behind leaders Oxford. Worse than we had ever imagined.

A snow-clearing operation involving volunteers got the home game with mighty Eastbourne Borough on – our first league action for four weeks.

Those wearing Luton replica tops with precious few layers underneath made a big mistake, for this proved one of the coldest 90 minutes I can remember at Kenilworth Road. I spent half-time striding briskly up and down behind the Main Stand simply to stay alive. In some form or another, I've been messing around in this same few square yards for around fifty years now; my very earliest memories involve playing in the various unedifying tunnels that run under the Main Stand as a toddler, while my dad stood on the terraces a few yards away watching the likes of Billy Bingham and Gordon Turner in action. There were crowds of around 20,000 most weeks back then, so it's a mystery how I was able to toddle off and then be easily reunited at the final whistle. Things were different back then, clearly.

Eastbourne brought ninety-two fans to the game, many missing the start due to traffic problems. Even with all present, there were still more folk in the executive boxes than in the entire away end. Home attendances were bearing up very well, but those empty seats at the Oak Road end constantly reminded us which league we were now in. Our humble visitors raised their game a few notches and looked full of purpose, taking a shock lead within 6 minutes. Thankfully, an equaliser arrived within 180 seconds, a first goal for Barnes-Homer. Gallen pounced minutes later and then grabbed a third before half-time. Points were precious, so Money tightened things up and left Gallen alone in attack. It raised the hackles of some fans, who couldn't fathom such negative tactics in a home game against part-timers. Jarvis conjured up a superb finish to make it 4-1 and all was well.

On New Year's Eve, we were able to sit back and reflect on one hell of a year at Kenilworth Road. Should we have raised a glass and remembered the (few) good bits, or should we have said good riddance and toasted a better future? Our outstanding April win at Wembley in front of 40,000 Luton fans was the undoubted highlight, but proved a temporary haven of happiness amid a sea of troubles. During the calendar year, Luton had played fifty-two times, winning twenty-one, drawing seventeen and losing fourteen. On paper it looked a reasonable record, but two-thirds of those victories came in non-League surroundings.

January 2010: All Human Emotion is Here

So to the FA Cup third-round day, which is still a top event on the football calendar, despite bigger clubs fielding weakened sides and television companies messing with kick-off times. This season we were getting used to the idea of Luton being non-League 'minnows' attempting to upset the bigger fish – and that meant middle-ranking League One side Southampton, who were forty-two rungs above the Hatters on the ladder. More than 3,000

Lutonians trekked to the South Coast. Media pundits discussing potential Cup shocks seemed to ignore this tie, which was quite comforting as it underlines my point about people not thinking of us as genuine minnows, despite our status at this time.

Hatters' fans sang 'Play up Pompey' to annoy the locals and generally enjoyed the change of scene. The pitch looked enormous, meaning our ball players could ping the ball about without Conference claustrophobia. We looked slick and confident early on, Craddock in particular. But after Nicholls left his mark on the slim frame of young Lallana, Lambert's free kick thundered into our net. Newton was guilty of an awful open-goal miss at the other end, and we duly exited the cup 1-0 as heroic failures.

The longest freeze-up to hit the UK in thirty years meant seven weeks with just one league game, although this was partly due to FA Trophy games mysteriously taking priority over the league. It left us at the season's halfway point trailing leaders Stevenage by seventeen points, but with four games in hand. The weather relented in time for a long trip to Gateshead's athletics stadium home, which holds around 12,000 but echoed to the cries of just 1,218 – 649 homesters and 569 Hatters. Fans clustered together and tried gamely to make some noise, but it felt more like a reserve game, with the players' shouts echoing around the ground. A highly forgettable occasion was decided by a comedy goal when Gnakpa's cross eluded embarrassed goalkeeper Farman.

Then came a more local excursion, to the frozen Cambridgeshire flatlands of Histon, complete with a brand-new giant centre-back in Janos Kovács (Hungarian for 'John Smith', according to Google). Luton management, with a hint of pride, claimed they beat the mighty Ferencvaros for his signature. Just short of 1,000 Luton fans rolled up (60 per cent of the entire gate), a good turnout on an absolutely filthy night. There was freezing sleet in the air and we longed for a comfortable covered stadium, not this exposed meadow in the Fens. The bitter cold meant numbed lips, frozen hands and consequently little noise. The atmosphere was so subdued one fan even reported hearing somebody drop some coins. When 'keeper Pilkington banged the soles of his boots on the post, in time-honoured fashion, the clanging echoed eerily around the ground.

Debutant Kovács dived to head a corner home in spectacular fashion. Cue the first real noise of the night and Kovács celebrated wildly – sprinting away, wild-eyed. The weather deteriorated further, but with Town looking dominant it was easier to take. Another Nicholls flag-kick swerved straight into the net, with maybe the slightest of touches from Hatch's head, but the referee disallowed the goal for reasons unknown.

The points were sewn up when Hall drilled home a firm shot. Nicholls imposed himself more as the game went on and was substituted to generous applause – and this time reciprocated after several weeks of giving us the silent treatment. We were all good friends again. This, in turn, raised an extra cheer.

Struggling Ebbsfleet (better known by former name Gravesend and Northfleet) visited Bedfordshire with Luton seeking a fourth successive league win for the first time since the heady days of 2005. Things began to go wrong early when 'keeper Pilkington hobbled off in pain, replaced by Gore for his league debut. After Hatch hammered us ahead, two episodes of sloppy defending allowed Brazilian Vieira to put the Kent side ahead before half-time. True to recent form, Luton fans were unwilling to be patient and the barracking began. Money was furious too, striding towards the tunnel well before the half-time whistle. Was he off home? Trying to beat the queue for a burger? Or maybe he wanted to be first in the dressing room to rehearse his half-time rocket?

Luton pulled level after the break when Asafu-Adjaye's long throw was bundled in by Craddock – but we shot ourselves in the foot again, giving away possession and falling 3-2 behind to Ashikodi's goal almost immediately. The odd defensive lapse is forgivable, but we'd now blundered three times in 25 minutes. When 'what a load of rubbish' rang out, Money applauded in the direction of the Kenilworth Road end, apparently signalling his agreement. If you like black humour, this man was certainly proving good value. As passionate and committed fans, we often stand accused of overreacting when things are going badly – and doing the same when things look good. Students of human behaviour would have had a field day at this game. Looking around, I saw rows of faces contorted with rage, anxiety and sheer pain. Others had gone completely blank. Blood vessels looked close to bursting in some cases. You'd never believe this was only a game of football. Luton being beaten 2-3 at home by Ebbsfleet was so patently absurd to some folk, they actually found themselves giggling. All human emotion was here.

Blogger David Mosque would later describe the moment rather neatly:

> I was so stunned I started to chuckle like a mad bloke. The scoreline was so shocking to my system that my psyche refused to accept it and so I started laughing like a fool. Perhaps my subconscious was protecting me from what should have been suicidal depression.

In the aftermath, some called this the club's lowest point ever and Money was in no mood to disagree, saying at the age of fifty-four he couldn't remember a moment in his entire career when he'd been more disappointed, angry and embarrassed.

February 2010: 'Get in My Son! Oh Deary, Deary Me!'

We were fully paid up non-Leaguers for six months now, but life down here still felt uncomfortable and alien. Oxford topped the table again, twelve points better off than Luton, who were marooned outside the play-off zone. Presumably for the sake of simply letting off some steam, one Luton fan set up a Facebook 'protest page' about our plight. He explained to the world,

> Five years ago Luton were holding their own against Wolves, West Brom, Stoke and Hull. Now, we're playing pub teams like Ebbsfleet, and worse still we're losing. The standard is so bad they don't even televise it. Instead we're reliant on shaky mobile videos on *YouTube*. I want us on *Match of the Day* again. I want proper football back, playing Charlton, not Crawley. Everton not Ebbsfleet.

Just a fortnight after January's 500-mile round trip to Gateshead, we tackled a 600-miler to Barrow. Holker Street ain't what it used to be, and that's saying something, for it never used to be much anyway. The loyal 302 who travelled were rewarded with uncovered terracing and thick fog (locals call it a 'sea fret'), but at least this was a proper football ground with classic old-style floodlight pylons and suchlike. One Hatters fan needed four trains and seven hours to get here, but felt it worthwhile. As a small boy, his prized possession had been a map of the ninety-two League grounds and he'd always wanted to do Barrow one day. Forty years later he made it. A little strip of card resembling a bus ticket got him into the ground. A friendly woman recorded the transaction in biro at her ancient turnstile. Welcome to the Conference.

The game was deadlocked, fog descending fast, but ten minutes from the end Hatch powered home a winner. It was a happy 300 miles home for the heroic 302. Despite the recent moaning and groaning, we hadn't been beaten on our travels in the league since September, nor conceded a single away goal since October. To still have any chance of sneaking that automatic promotion place, however, Oxford would have to be put to the sword three days later at Kenilworth Road.

It was a bitterly cold Tuesday night, but the atmosphere was red- hot. Craddock smacked the crossbar but Oxford broke through late on with a scrambled goal against the run of play. Our pain was acute, but deadened by a dramatic surge of relief in stoppage time when a Keane corner was headed in by Pilkington. People leaving the ground were stopped in their tracks by the noise, and Oxford looked shell-shocked. And Luton were not finished yet. At least 95 minutes' play had ticked by when we won another corner on the same side. Keane ran over again.

The next few moments are seared indelibly in the memory. And, fortunately, captured for posterity by a wonderful piece of radio commentary by Luton fan Simon 'Statto' Pitts, working for community station Diverse FM. A clip of it went viral the next day. When reading this transcript, imagine you are slowly turning a volume switch a notch higher with each sentence...

> Keane's racing over. He'll take the corner kick. Oxford have all eleven men in the box once more. Luton have all men forward except Newton on the edge of the centre circle. Keane curls it into the far post. It's in! IT'S IN! Keith Keane has scored direct from a corner. Keith Keane for the Hatters! It's 2-1. Get in my son! You beauty! Oh, this is brilliant! Oh, can you believe it! Keith Keane has scored direct from the corner – I'm sure of it! Oh, unbelievable! Oh deary, deary me! If I bust your eardrums I make no apologies, the Hatters have turned it around in injury time! Oh, unbelievable. Oh, what a fantastic, fantastic performance...

Kenilworth Road was in the sort of uproar not seen since Ahmet Brkovic's late winner flattened Hull in a crucial League One tussle a few years ago. Perfect strangers hugged each other, people leapt dangerously across tip-up seats, and others stumbled and fell ecstatically on narrow concrete walkways. Many missed the sight of Keane being sent off apparently for 'over-celebrating'. This ridiculous decision was jobsworth officialdom at its best. Keane had been next to the corner flag and was simply swamped by nearby fans. As he slowly barrelled off (he's not the most elegant of movers), he received a massive ovation. Grown men bade him farewell, singing 'There's only one Keano', tears of joy in their eyes.

Within seconds of the restart the whistle went, Keane still barely having reached the tunnel. Oxford couldn't believe they'd been 1-0 up on 93 minutes and still lost. Neither could we. Neither could AFC Wimbledon manager Terry Brown, who left on 90 minutes and was in his car and away, thinking Oxford had won. Even if everything else was to go pear-shaped this season, we knew we'd had at least one golden moment to remember.

Life proved less hectic the following weekend at snowbound Eastbourne, where volunteers with forks and wheelbarrows got the pitch playable. The little ground looked isolated in the corner of a huge field, not far from the beach. A mind-blowing thought: during our last spell in football's top flight in the 1980s, Eastbourne were playing village teams in Division Three of the Sussex County League. Quaint military band music greeted the teams' arrival on the pitch, followed by a verbose PA announcer, who turned out to be well informed and went into great detail about the history of Luton. There was more in the programme, including a theory over why Luton folk are known for dropping the 'T' when it occurs in the middle of a word (as in the chant 'Come on Lu-on'). It's not simply because we speak Estuary English in our part of the world, it's due to thousands of hat workers in the town chattering while gripping straw in their mouths, consequently unable to pronounce their Ts. An interesting theory, but utter tosh surely?

We looked positive in the early stages, Hall cracking home a daisy-cutter to put us ahead. The stands were low and the ball regularly sailed into nearby meadows. I wondered if anybody had ever reached the beach from here? It was a pity John Dreyer wasn't still marshalling our defence, for he would have had a crack at it. Barnes-Homer changed his awful yellow boots to something a little more tasteful at half-time, but it failed to yield more goals. However, another clean sheet meant we'd now exceeded 700 minutes since conceding. Seven wins from eight games and the seventh successive away clean sheet is a club record. Real progress at last?

In contrast to the 'village team made good' at Eastbourne, three days later we headed north to tackle a famous name fallen on hard times. York City were four points ahead of us, and an altogether sterner challenge. They'd struggled to achieve 3,000 crowds for most games, but remained a noisy bunch who went in for flags and tickertape. Perhaps most enthusiastic of all was Dr John Sentamu, the Archbishop of York, closely involved in various activities behind the scenes at the Kit Kat Stadium. Around 60 tons of sand had been put on the pitch recently, which helped ensure our game was no classic. A goalless draw ended York's winning run, but a disgruntled Money compared the pitch to Blackpool beach.

Home again, and nearly 8,000 witnessed the visit of the real Wimbledon (as opposed to the manufactured franchise version in Milton Keynes), who displayed those party pooper qualities the original club were famous for. Elder's effort crept over our goalline ahead of the scrambling Tyler in such slow motion the away fans took ages to register they'd actually scored. Craddock poached a quick equaliser, but on the hour mark Kedwell swooped to win it. Invincible away from home, we had now lost five on home turf. The visitors raved about the greatest result in their short history, in front of the biggest crowd ever to watch them.

It was a serious blow to our title hopes, and although the boo-boys were relatively subdued at the end, one fan's comments angered Money, who darted across and confronted him eyeball to eyeball, much to the alarm of the stewards. Next day, MD Gary Sweet urged forbearance:

We've set ourselves a target to learn in one year what it has taken others five. Of course, we'd love to win every game but must realise we won't. Occasionally, we must detach performance from result and not simply think we are crap if we lose, or brilliant if we win.

A few interesting stats were emerging; for example, Luton's average league crowd was around the 7,000 mark, i.e. better or on a par with at least forty of the ninety-two League clubs. Not bad for a club fifth in the Conference. Chairmen from the Conference clubs met this month and, as expected, mismanaged Chester were kicked out of the league and points won against them would be struck off. There was delight among Hatters fans because despised local promotion rivals Stevenage lost six points as a result; we only lost two. But there was widespread sympathy for Chester fans. Their tale of woe was horrendous; they'd recently appointed a former Sunday League manager with a criminal record as 'director of football'. A fans' action group was said to be ensuring that 125 years of history didn't die by creating a newly constituted club from the ashes.

Crawley away was next, and from all accounts they were vacuuming the red carpet in readiness. Their local paper asked readers:

> Have Reds ever been involved in a bigger match than the tussle with Luton? Be honest, what was the first fixture you looked up when they came out last summer? Eastbourne? No, it would have been the visit of the big clubs, the ex-Football League outfits like Oxford, Cambridge, Wimbledon and – the biggest of them all – Luton.

More than 1,000 Hatters assembled in the relatively roomy away sections. The 2,118 crowd was easily Crawley's best of the season, and we were only forty-seven short of making up half of it. But the game was a poor spectacle. After an uneventful first half, Nicholls was robbed in a dangerous area and Smith finished clinically. After 852 minutes without conceding an away goal, we were behind. Minutes later, Nicholls departed down the tunnel with a face like thunder. Much later it became clear why: his chronic injuries had beaten him, and a brilliant Luton career was finished. Barnes-Homer responded to some pointless barracking by smashing a fine equaliser, and briefly we looked strong and confident. It didn't last. Poor defending allowed Smith an 87th-minute winner. Over in the dugouts, Money didn't rant and rave, he just slumped back into a semi-recline, looking utterly flabbergasted. He wasn't the only one.

March 2010: Grassy Terracing, Corrugated Iron Stands

The axe fell on four players after Crawley. The reshuffle heralded a workmanlike display at Mansfield, which ended goalless, although recalled Howells had what appeared a perfectly good goal disallowed. With barely time to draw breath it was then off to Hayes. This suburb is just 13 miles west of Charing

Cross, but miraculously I found free parking next to a well-preserved little rustic church. It was unexpectedly relaxed and bucolic – squirrels frolicked, birds twittered in the sunshine and belching Luton fans wandered past with chips and Coke.

Hayes is where Ray Wilkins and Greg Dyke grew up, and home for a spell to author George Orwell. Orwell hated his time here, lampooning the place under another name in at least two of his books. The football club is a recent amalgamation of the Hayes and Yeading clubs, but they operated in an old-fashioned, traditional ground, complete with crumbling old concrete terracing and crush barriers. Two thirds of the crowd of 1,881 were Luton fans, and our presence attracted a noisy rabble of about twenty-five yobs, who, it transpired, were actually QPR fans looking for trouble. Police were tipped off they'd be here and dealt with them. Luton were a class above the homesters throughout, but could never entirely relax. A Hatch header, Gnakpa penalty and Craddock special were answered by two home goals, but the 3-2 win was far more emphatic than it sounds.

Chester confirmed they wouldn't be appealing their expulsion and their 2009/10 results were formally expunged. The resultant changes to the league table left us in the play-off zone (fifth) and a little nearer the top. It was probably Luton's first lucky break since the downward spiral began several years ago – for those 0-0 draws at home and away to Chester were probably our worst performances of the season, and both were consigned to the dustbin. They wouldn't appear in the record books and we could pretend they had never happened. We now had twelve games left, eight at home, and were nine points off the top. A degree of optimism returned.

It was starting to feel as if the wretched winter had lasted for ever, and the visit of Forest Green proved another bone-chiller. Luton dominated but lacked ruthlessness where it counted. Barnes-Homer was jeered when substituted, reminding us of the general discontent that was still bubbling away. It hadn't been helping much, for players' heads had been dropping when the moaning started. Craddock netted a penalty only for Kovács to concede one after falling to the ground. It didn't look deliberate but it brought an equaliser. The tiny band of forty-two away fans celebrated this unexpected good fortune, one racing on the pitch only to be instantly thrown out for his trouble. Disgruntled Luton fans sang 'this is embarrassing' at the prospect of another draw. It looked like two points had gone west until the 90th minute, when Craddock forced the ball home amid vain claims he handled. Relieved Luton unashamedly played the ball into the corners to kill time and the whistle signalled a great outcome, if not a great performance. We rose to third, rivals Oxford, York and AFC Wimbledon all having lost.

Money told his critics the condition of the pitch was preventing flowing football and offered a guided tour of the playing surface to any doubters.

Nobody took him up on this, I understand, but there was a fast response when 2,800 tickets were snapped up for the Stevenage trip at Easter, three weeks hence. This brand-new local derby caught the imagination big time. With bad weather and cup competitions creating a winter period of eighty-three days with only four league games completed, we faced a crowded fixture list to the end of the season. A run of twenty-three games in ninety-one days was underway – one that, with hindsight, would prove a very fruitful spell. Pivotal had been the arrival of hard-working Simon Heslop from Barnsley to replace Nicholls, who was having his knee rebuilt again.

The horror show at Wrexham the previous autumn was put to bed when the return game saw a fine first-half display starring Heslop and Keane. Craddock went on a run and clouted a real cracker to put us ahead. Wrexham hit the bar after the interval and we had to hang on desperately. There was light relief when Keane attempted to take a corner, but somehow kicked the flag instead. The impact caused him to stagger sideways like a drunk parading down George Street; the crowd was in stitches and fortunately Keano saw the funny side too. Three good points were won but, as fans and players applauded each other, the manager marched off staring at the ground and covering his ears with his hands. If this gesture was meant to be humorous, it rather backfired, for it sparked much discussion over the next day or two. One wag even called the debate 'Eargate'. Opinion swung between Money being impressively feisty, or simply childish. Meanwhile, an explanation emerged for Barnes-Homer's recent lack of confidence and form – his father Ken had died after a short battle with cancer. The boo-boys felt a bit differently after this, and one fan's website even issued an apology.

The third home game in eight days saw Kidderminster under the cosh as Howells hooked a spectacular goal – only his second in more than fifty games – and minutes later, Gallen netted a low drive. Lawrie pulled one back but Gallen sped into the box, cut inside and cracked home a classy effort to seal a 3-1 win. Late sub Barnes-Homer got a tremendous ovation in recognition of his recent bereavement. We were now just a couple of points off the top and a genuine title challenge was on. The meeting with Stevenage a fortnight hence would be massive. Things were panning out a little more like we'd always hoped. But had we left it too late? Money certainly thought not, telling the media our promotion rivals were 'messing their pants' over Luton's recent form. He based this on news that several clubs were appealing the decision to take away the points everybody gained against recently expelled Chester.

Across the Thames into Kent to tackle Ebbsfleet, a club run for two years by internet venture myfootballclub.co.uk. Fans bought shares to become joint owners, allowing them a vote on all aspects of the club, including team selection. However, a slump in membership saw budgets slashed and manager Liam Daish's rebuilt side were finding times tough.

Their 105-year-old home, on a cold, grey, damp afternoon, had bags of old-fashioned charm. Even more so when contrasted with the steel and glass of nearby Ebbsfleet Eurostar terminal. Ancient terracing, grass growing between the cracks, crush barriers with multi-layered coats of red-and-white paint and patched-up corrugated iron roofs to the stands. It felt like a trip back to the 1960s.

Some enthusiastic stewards gave Luton fans a good frisking. Didn't they know our main offensive weapon (Kevin Nicholls) was not present that day? Once inside, Kent police got up close and personal with video cameras, but at least we were spared the helicopter buzzing overhead. Halfway through the first period, Kovács lost his bearings and slid the ball comically into his own net. It rolled so slowly Tyler seemed to have time to do a triple pike and salco before getting back, but arrived a split second too late. It was against the run of play and was the only way Ebbsfleet were going to score. Thankfully a second-half display of clinical finishing turned the contest on its head. Luton banged in no fewer than six, five of them in 28 minutes. It was the type of landslide we'd been waiting for all season. Gnakpa was the unlikely hat-trick man, heading the equaliser from a corner then thrashing home two shots within 60 seconds. He looked so fired up when wheeling away in celebration, it appeared he was about to run straight for the Eurostar terminal over the road, to tell friends and family back in France what he'd done. Clinical finishes by Craddock and Gallen meant we were soon coasting at 5-1. Barnes-Homer was cheered on as a late sub, the loss of his father having reversed his anti-hero status. Appropriately, he slotted the sixth goal, running to the crowd and getting mobbed in a lengthy love-in that resulted in him being booked. Craddock scoffed at the referee for such a petty gesture, and he too had a yellow card brandished in his face.

This display of jobsworthiness ensured we had no sympathy when the official was knocked senseless by a clearance hitting him squarely on the side of the head. It raised a loud cheer as he started to wobble, tumbling down like the ref in the infamous Paolo di Canio incident. But he managed a sharp blast on the whistle to stop the game before hitting the ground!

We'd achieved what looked well-nigh impossible a few weeks ago by overhauling Oxford – who were once fifteen points ahead – and were now second, two points behind Stevenage, albeit having played two games more. Money responded by attending a supporters' club social event and was warmly received. He showed another side to the tetchy, stern-faced fellow we'd come to know, and many people came away with a less critical view.

Just a week after bashing six goals in the second half, we chalked up seven in the first period at home to Hayes and Yeading. Without wishing to over-egg the stats, I think scoring thirteen goals in a 76-minute passage of play deserves a mention. We're not likely to see that happen again soon. Luton went 7-0 up in 35 minutes, seemingly finding the net every time they moved forward. We fans got greedy and started dreaming of exceeding the club record of 12-0 created in the 1930s, but ultimately had to settle for just the eight. However, it was the first eight-goal haul in my lifetime – the last occasion was against Sunderland, just four days before I was born in 1955.

Gallen had got things moving by picking his spot before setting up Gnakpa for a second. A lovely move was finished by Gnapka for 3-0 on 13 minutes, the fourth soon following as Gallen converted Craddock's pass. Keane intercepted a clearance to curl in the next, and Craddock's header made it six. Gallen was visibly gobsmacked at being deprived of his first-ever hat-trick when a shot hit both posts, stayed out and was tapped in by Howells. The other players found this hilarious. Luckily, the electronic scoreboard kept pace, for without it we'd surely have lost count. Ironic chants of 'boring, boring Luton' were heard as we went a full 10 minutes without further goals!

Poor Hayes restored a modicum of pride, conceding just once after the break when Craddock chipped against a post, collected the rebound and casually converted. Sub Hatch missed a couple of golden chances to make it 10-0. In a stroke, we had virtually wiped out Oxford's better goal difference, and could take pleasure from all eight being pure footballing goals, arising from open play and not set pieces. A scoreline of 8-0 was a splendid way to start the first of eight games in a twenty-eight-day period to complete the season. Confidence was sky-high. One explanation for the recent goal rush was the special soup being made by Gnakpa's mum. He'd recently been sent a substantial supply of Mrs Gnakpa's speciality – a sort of fusion broth. We were told he'd been necking large quantities of this stuff and had plenty more in the freezer of his Bedford home for future use.

A 'mere' four goals found Salisbury City's net a few days later, but some spells of Luton attacking were as good as anything seen since the mid-Mike Newell era. Moderate opposition, yes, but you can't argue against eighteen goals scored in a passage of 210 minutes of play. It was now seven wins in a row, with twenty-seven goals scored, leaving us firmly in second spot, five points behind Stevenage, who beat Oxford that night. Salisbury were made to look very ordinary. Gnakpa rose and headed a fine goal in off the bar, Craddock converted a simple chance and was responsible for setting up Howells and Heslop to round things off. March had been one hell of a month – it started with Luton fifth and twelve points behind Oxford, and a goal difference inferior by nineteen. Thirty days later, we were second, three points ahead of them, and with a better goal difference.

April 2010: A Life-Size Blow-Up Doll Called Roger

Who says the French have no sense of humour? That Gallic scamp Gnakpa had another chuckle at our expense that month. Barely had the excitement died down about his soup revelations before he was posting on Facebook that he'd signed for hometown club Olympique Marseilles. News of this transfer failed to appear elsewhere, so it was no surprise when a few hours later he came clean and revealed it to be an April Fool's prank.

Meanwhile, all roads pointed to the big derby at Stevenage, technically not a title decider, but almost being treated as such, the biggest crowd in the Lamex Stadium's history in prospect. As the crow flies, the clubs are separated by 10 miles, but in terms of history and fanbase they are poles apart. It's hard to believe so much tension and anticipation can surround a non-League fixture. Parts of Britain's first designated new town rang to the sound of 'Top of the league, you're having a laugh' as the invading army arrived. Superfan John Pyper had a huge banner declaring 'Dickie Dosh's Barmy Army', and he assured me the manager didn't mind us using this nickname, having got that directly from the horse's mouth.

It was good to see we were all pulling in the same direction, and during the game I even spotted managing director Sweet slumming it on the East Terrace instead of luxuriating in the director's box. We needed the points for obvious reasons, but to win would be all the sweeter in view of Stevenage's general approach to the beautiful game. This was typified by an incident in the first half, when Odubade hit the floor, apparently mortally wounded. The physio was called for. Immediately, manager Westley organised a basketball-style 'timeout'. All his players except Odubade and the goalkeeper rushed over for a tactics talk and drink. Coming after exactly 30 minutes, this was clearly pre-arranged. The officials did nothing about it. Luton fans and management were furious. Money stood there giving a mocking 'timeout' signal, and coach Watson attempted to have it broken up, but the fourth official seemed too intimidated to take action.

Worse things happen on a football field, of course, but when you add this to the rest of Stevenage's catalogue of gamesmanship, you can see why they were so unpopular. Roberts, their towering, bleached-blond centre-half and captain, was constantly in the ref's ear, and fond of racing 50 yards to remonstrate over incidents in which he wasn't involved. Stevenage made a point of disrupting the rhythm of the game by just about any means possible. In the second half, their ballboys disappeared altogether, a mysterious move that Stevenage clearly thought would help them.

It was a typical local derby, and Money got his tactics just right. Gallen and Craddock saw little of the ball at their feet in the first half, so the former was withdrawn and target-man Hatch joined the fray. Craddock departed in favour of Barnes-Homer. The latter was involved immediately, forcing a throw on the left. Murray found Howells, who lost possession, but Stevenage failed to clear. Hatch challenged and the loose ball fell to Barnes-Homer, who half-volleyed it high into the net, a mere 50 seconds after his arrival. Cue mass celebrations and general acknowledgement that Dickie Dosh was a tactical genius. Westley, bless him, later claimed the goal was a 'miskick'. No wonder the *Daily Telegraph* described him as 'David Brent from *The Office* on speed'.

The goal increased the friction in the dugouts, and Stevenage coach Maamria was sent to the stands for extreme behaviour. Luton absorbed everything the league leaders could muster, and it was clear this was no longer the Luton team of old who would buckle under late pressure. All the motivational slogans in the world couldn't get Stevenage a goal today. It left us two points behind them, having played a game more. They remained title favourites, but what a turnaround since the end of February.

Gallen had made his professional debut sixteen years earlier against Manchester United, and has been scoring goals ever since. But he saved his very first hat-trick for Easter 2010 against the hapless Grays. It ended 6-0 and could have been far more – we hit the woodwork twice, Howells had a brilliant solo goal unluckily ruled out, and two goal-bound headers by Gnakpa were well saved. A brace by poacher Craddock and a Hatch diving header completed the scoring. Gallen was watched for the first time by young daughters Sofia and Siena. He gave them a fatherly wave after completing his hat-trick, but sadly they were too busy on their Nintendo DS to notice. Not since Manchester United played Barnsley in the Premier League had there been a bigger gulf between two clubs in the same division. Luton, with their much-envied squad, were being cheered on by nearly 8,000 people, and nearly skint Grays, struggling to even fill their eleven shirts, had twenty-one fans looking on.

The table showed Stevenage needing eleven points from their final five games to ensure we could not catch them. Money, who had just won Manager of the Month, was heard on local radio sounding irritated again. Turned out he'd detected a few moans from fans when we reached the 30-minute mark against Grays with the scoresheet still blank. Perhaps he should have considered reducing the oxygen of publicity he kept giving the whingers.

We headed up to Tamworth, finding the locals a bit grumpy at being ousted from their usual standing areas in The Shed to allow for the sheer volume of the visiting Luton support. They got even more down when Pilkington headed us in front. Veteran Des Lyttle scuffed an equaliser to foil our bid to chalk up a tenth successive win. At the final whistle, there was a definite sense of anti-climax. Gone was our last realistic chance of winning the Conference title. Stevenage beat Forest Green the same day and it would have taken a major collapse to let us back in now. Play-offs it was to be then. Our problem had been hitting form too late in the day. If we'd accelerated into peak form by February, rather than March, things would have been different.

The date 13 April is one that means goals all the way at Luton Town. On this day in 1936, we lashed twelve past Bristol Rovers and now, seventy-four years later, another half-dozen were netted against mid-table Histon. It was the fourth time in twenty-four days we'd hit somebody for six, but the evening was tarnished a little by the visitors managing three. Nevertheless, credit to The Stutes for playing an open game and not piling men behind the ball like most other Confererence opponents. Craddock followed Gallen's example with the first senior hat-trick of his career, Howells grabbed a couple, and Gallen got his eighteenth of the season. Two of the three pulled back by Histon in the final 20 minutes were cracking efforts; the last by Southam even winning applause from home fans.

Our last home game before the play-offs saw Altrincham 'park the bus' and keep out seventeen shots and nine corners to grind out a goalless draw. Simultaneously, Stevenage won at Kidderminster to be confirmed as champions, taking the only automatic promotion place. Luton's league programme ended with a visit to Rushden and Diamonds for a dead rubber game, both sides already assured of play-off places. A remarkable 2,797 away fans still travelled though, mostly in mellow mood, carrying plastic bags of food and soft drinks in the sunshine. It was what commentators like to call 'a shirt-sleeved crowd'.

Some opted for traditional end-of-season fancy dress, one middle-aged chap apparently depicting a member of Sgt Pepper's Lonely Hearts Club Band. There was a female Hatter sporting what looked like a baseball umpire's outfit, although it was far too revealing to pass for an accurate copy. There were curly orange wigs, balloons, a beach ball, and even a life-size plastic blow-up doll. Unexpectedly, the doll turned out to be a male named Roger, who was in a state of arousal until the unrelenting sun and 3,000 pairs of hands led to partial deflation. When smiting the plastic inflatables into the air became boring, conga dancing ensued. The baseball umpire proved a popular figure to cling on to. The police and stewards wisely stood back and let it all go. Lutonians always like to have fun on 24 April – it's the anniversary of our 1988 League Cup win, you see. An early goal by Craddock was quickly cancelled out by Byrne's equaliser, which he unwisely celebrated right in front of us. It ended all square and with Oxford losing at Eastbourne; Luton were confirmed as runners-up for the season and would face York in the play-off semi-finals.

Optimism was not dampened by the torrential rain that accompanied the advance of the Luton army up the A1 towards the battlements of York for the Thursday night confrontation. Arriving at the city's outer suburbs, the first face I saw was a familiar one, a bloke who sits near me at Kenilworth Road supping a pint, minding his own business and watching the world go by from a pub called the Old Grey Mare. It was comforting to know that fellow Lutonians had pierced enemy ranks and were happily in position well before kick-off. The start was delayed due to traffic congestion as 6,204 squeezed into the old ground. It was a decent-sized crowd for non-League football, but York still opted for artificial methods to crank up the atmosphere. Sections of the home support obediently waved red flags in unison, streamers were thrown on from behind the goal and a clown with a megaphone danced around madly. Most of us visitors got drenched to the skin on an open terrace. All rather grim, but there was a whiff of nostalgia about it – or was that just the ancient toilets?

It was an open game with Luton looking in good shape and doing everything right except scoring. Both sides struck the woodwork, a first-leg goalless draw was starting to look a decent result until suddenly Shane Blackett made his only slip of the game late on, allowing prolific Brodie a clear path on goal to make it 1-0. It was a real sickener, but had been a good game in the conditions, considerably more entertaining than the dross served up 48 hours earlier on television by Barcelona and Inter Milan in a deadlocked Champions League semi-final. There was an inevitability about Brodie being the villain of the piece. This baby-faced assassin, all shaved head and ruddy cheeks, wound Luton fans up by appealing for everything, hitting the floor too easily and moaning at officials. Defeat was all the more galling having finished the season three places and ten points higher than York, with twenty-two more goals scored.

The only laughs came during the performance at pitchside by York fan Dr John Sentamu (the Most Revd and Rt Hon. Lord Archbishop of York), who shouted far too loudly into the microphone and ended his surreal contribution with 'hip hip hooray' and other inanities. Luton used to count the Archbishop of Canterbury Dr Robert Runcie among our regular fans, but he made far less noise than his York counterpart.

May 2010: A Cauldron of Frustration

It was a nervy build-up to the second leg at Luton. Needing to overcome a 1-0 deficit increased the pressure. Fans were in turmoil: Angie hadn't felt like this since the big Maine Road showdown in Manchester, twenty-seven years earlier; Yvette said her stomach was churning and she'd hardly slept; Jane said she'd pretend for as long as possible it was just an ordinary day, and urged anyone with a better coping mechanism to get in touch urgently;

Pete said he'd been pacing nervously around the house and would pacify himself with a fry-up; Namhatter reckoned days like these turned a man to drink, so he also planned a big fry-up first. He promised he'd wear his lucky pants to the game, though.

There was a near full house of 9,781 gathered and a place at Wembley at stake. York were in the driving seat after the first leg, and we fretted that our wonderful six-week purple patch (eleven wins and forty-one goals) could now be a case of peaking too soon, rather than too late. Inevitably, the game proved a tense struggle in the sun, York resolute and well drilled. Half-time came and went without the breakthrough we needed, and shortly after the restart a fierce Rankine free-kick was parried by Tyler for Carruthers to net the rebound. Cue that awful, sickening silence we last experienced when Stevenage were here the previous autumn. Two-up on aggregate and York looked far too organised to crumble now, and so it proved. It was the first-leg goal that really killed us. We were left to agonise over the fact the play-off final at Wembley would be between York and Oxford, teams we finished well clear of.

So the season ended in a cauldron of frustration. Newton was sent off in the closing minutes for dissent, and there was a pitch invasion at the end by 500 or so – a small number of whom went looking for trouble. Coins and other small missiles were hurled in the direction of York players and fans celebrating at the Oak Road end. As the tunnel could not be safely reached, stewards ushered the York team into an unoccupied area of seats, where they were assailed by more small missiles. The possibility of being trapped by an angry mob turned the players' smiles into expressions of panic before they were hurriedly pushed through a rear exit. It was never the full-scale riot it would later be portrayed as, and the missile-throwers were small in number, but clearly it was the last thing our club needed on its biggest match day of the season. One media person suggested this episode might help scupper England's bid to host the World Cup, which was plainly laughable.

York boss Foyle sympathised with Luton ('the best side in the league, football wise'), and at the subsequent Wembley final won by Oxford, Wrexham boss Dean Saunders banged the drum on television for two clubs to be automatically promoted from the Conference in future. He said there was a bottleneck of clubs with big fanbases unable to get out and replace the half-dozen or so League Two sides who, on paper at least, were much weaker outfits. Quite.

2

2010/11 Season

August 2010: A Frank Exchange of Opinions

Another season commenced in the footballing wilderness, but Richard Money showed Luton meant business by adding eight signings to the squad, and flying everyone to Portugal to bond and get fit in the sun. Back in Luton, the club's 125th anniversary prompted creation of a commemorative 'retro' playing kit of pink and blue, to be worn for the opening game at home to Altincham. In August the air was warm, the grass was green and the hope springs eternal.

We moved smoothly into gear, impressive new Czech centre-back Zdenek Kroca heading the first goal of the campaign. For the next 50 minutes or so, chance after chance went begging and, predictably, Altrincham drew level with their first effort on target. It was head in hands time. But, right at the death, after debutant Danny Crow went close with a diving header, Barnes-Homer netted a thunderous 20-yarder. All was well with the world.

We were still on course a few days later with a 3-1 win at Kettering. Luton old boy Roper ploughed into Gallen, allowing Barnes-Homer to net from the spot, but minutes later, Christie was left unmarked to equalise. In the final 20 minutes the fun really started, with Christie and Roper sent off and Barnes-Homer completing a hat-trick, including another penalty. It was even better the following weekend when Fleetwood were flattened 3-0 on their own turf – Barnes-Homer sweeping in an early goal, quickly followed by Gnakpa rounding the 'keeper for a second. Defender Linwood departed after two yellow cards, and 715 travelling fans were in fine voice. Craddock, surprisingly only a sub, came on and rounded things off with a far-post header.

Newly promoted Newport's credentials were tested to the full at Kenilworth Road the following Tuesday, but they grabbed a shock lead when winger Henry rifled home a beauty. Kroca, who along with ex-Stevenage midfielder Andy Drury was looking an excellent capture, poked in an equaliser minutes later. The second half was again Luton-dominated but chances were wasted, and Barnes-Homer even fluffed a penalty. Newport employed spoiling tactics, and Keane was red-carded as the desperate hunt for a winner went unrewarded. Many fans were glum-faced, even though we were top of the table.

With the 100 per cent record gone, the next slice of bad news was that Kevin Nicholls was finished. After more than 200 appearances, our thirty-one-year-old uncompromising captain agreed a cancellation of his contract after accepting his battle-scarred knee would never allow him to scale the heights of his first golden spell at Luton. Taking a wage while not contributing much to the cause was apparently bugging him, so tearing up his contract was an admirable gesture in this otherwise greedy world. It wouldn't be the same without him, and there were emotional scenes at the club as he reluctantly departed.

Bad luck comes in threes, and this nasty little week ended with angry scenes at Tamworth, following a miserable 1-3 defeat. Perry nodded them ahead early, and we played second fiddle until the second period when Craddock fired an equaliser. Midfielder Pavel Besta, struggling to adapt to new surroundings, misplaced a pass and allowed the Lambs to regain the lead. The poor Czech got dog's abuse from some Luton fans for this, and Money was clearly furious at such a reaction. The atmosphere got even worse when Bradley swooped to seal the home victory. The hostility from Luton fans behind the dugout tipped Money over the edge. After the final whistle, to the horror of colleagues, he remonstrated wildly with the fans, and had to be held back as the row escalated. As he was pulled away and shepherded toward the exit, he was roundly booed from elsewhere in the ground and started gesticulating in response. The provocation was certainly severe, but to see a manager react like this was shocking. He was clearly furious over a number of things, the barracking of Besta proving the final straw.

The fans involved in this frank exchange of opinions, and some who just happened to be in that general area, were quick to post their views on social media, and a clip of the tirade appeared on YouTube. Money issued an apology the following day that stretched to nearly 500 words and included the following:

> I allowed my frustrations to get the better of me and most certainly shouldn't have done so. The last few days at the club have been very emotional. For everyone to see someone leave [Nicholls] after such a long period of committed service was upsetting. When I heard some of the things being directed at our players I wrongly erupted instead of ignoring it, as I should have done. I suppose it touched a nerve and brought to the forefront of my mind when even Nicholls was verbally abused by a minority when he was

playing through pain by those who considered him a legend. It reminded me of when some were being over critical of Barnes-Homer without giving him a chance and when his father was gravely ill. Yesterday, I had a brand new player [Besta] trying his damnedest, in a scrappy game in a foreign environment to him so I snapped when I should have been bigger and more professional.

He insisted Luton Town remained very important to him: 'I love it here and I'm 100 per cent committed and confident that we are capable of winning this league this season, starting tomorrow at home to Hayes and Yeading.' The apology came over as genuine, and there was belated sympathy for Besta, said to be distraught over his mistake and the reaction it provoked – and also some for Money himself, whose outburst at least proved he cared intensely about losing to what was frankly rather ordinary opposition.

With lowly placed part-timers Hayes and Yeading paying us a visit on the Bank Holiday just 48 hours later, there was a great opportunity for the bad atmosphere to be quickly banished. As impatient fans, we naturally insisted that the lesser lights of the Conference must be well beaten at home if a serious title challenge was to be mounted. And, of course, only a few months ago we had hit Hayes and Yeading for eight, so what was the problem? But life, and football, is not that simple.

Inevitably, the visitors fed off the anxiety and looked far more confident and well organised than on their last appearance here. Tyler had to make a sensational save to keep them out in a goalless first half. Suitably encouraged, they started the second period strongly, taking a shock lead when Pritchard lofted a shot home after Tyler's punch went straight to him. Luton's turmoil intensified, but the response was good; Keane's free-kick slipped home at the far post by Drury. Penalty claims were turned down and a Kroca header rattled the bar as we chased a winner that never came. Adding to the misery, Drury was dismissed for a second bookable offence. To put it mildly, the 1-1 scoreline was not well received by the 6,354, less than 100 of whom were visitors.

The month of August ended grimly both on and off the field. Popular striker Craddock, last year's leading scorer with twenty-four, departed for Oxford on deadline day for £50,000, which was £30,000 less than we paid for this young prospect. The news didn't go down well, although he couldn't be blamed for wanting League football – especially as he'd been sub in four of our opening six games, and hadn't been called upon during the failure to beat Hayes and Yeading. Barely a year earlier, the *Daily Mail* had referred to his move to Luton from Middlesbrough as one of the best fifty signings of that year by any British club.

September 2010:
Three Penalties Missed in Five Minutes

Live television coverage of the contest at Grimsby dictated a Saturday evening kick-off, but the change of routine failed to galvanise Town and the winless run stretched to four as we succumbed 2-0, despite striking the woodwork twice. The manager urged us to stay patient and not start panicking as league tables didn't mean much until after Christmas. Just as well then, for we'd dropped below the play-off zone. To fill the Craddock void, well-travelled Kenyan international Taiwo Atieno returned for a second spell at the club.

To huge relief all round, some semblance of momentum was regained with two home wins in six days. The first was 2-0 over Cambridge, Drury curling in a smart goal and setting up Pilkington's vital second. An impressive turnout of 7,283 then watched league leaders AFC Wimbledon trounced 3-0, another game screened live by the Premier Sports channel. First-half headers by Pilkington and Kroca got the crowd going, and Barnes-Homer's drive polished off the Wombles' challenge shortly after the restart. Drury's suspension and Keane's injury saw defender Pilkington play central midfield alongside young Howells, one of many permutations to be tried out in the engine room this season.

After the warm intimacy of a packed Kenilworth Road, the lads undertook two marathon trips up north to the draughty underpopulated stadiums that Darlington and Gateshead call home. More than 200 Lutonians arrived at the Darlington Arena on a brisk Tuesday evening and were rewarded when Gnakpa headed in Drury's early cross, just moments after the same pair combined to strike the crossbar. Atieno almost made it two, before ex-Hatter Hatch headed the Quakers level. Brown's drive then found the Luton net through a sea of bodies, and Money had just 10 minutes to repair the damage. He threw on a forward for a defender with instant success, Howells taking Newton's pass, making space and firing a deserved equaliser.

The athletics stadium at Gateshead was attended by barely 1,000 souls five days later, and it felt like much of the good work of recent weeks was spoiled as we went down to a miserable 1-0 defeat in the uninspiring surroundings. Early dominance by Ian Bogie's side culminated in Shaw heading home. Things got worse when a challenge by Atieno was harshly red carded before half-time (later rescinded). Money made tactical switches and used all his subs, including a debut for Bedford youngster Dan Walker, but to no avail. A thoroughly depressing day, but the Bogie man celebrated 'the finest win of [his] managerial career'.

Luton now languished in seventh, underachieving in the eyes of pretty much everybody, even the pragmatists. We were five points behind current leaders, little Crawley Town. When we tumbled into this non-League abyss, we naturally expected the likes of Wrexham, Grimsby, Oxford, Mansfield and York to be providing the most serious opposition at the top end of the table, but eighteen months after demotion we found ourselves hanging on the coat-tails of minnows Crawley. Yes, Crawley.

How could these uncelebrated Sussex minnows, with a recent history of major off-field troubles, be topping the Conference? To put it simply, the reason was money. Lots of it. Earlier that year, boyhood fan Bruce Winfield, finance director of a marketing group, announced he and two business partners had become majority shareholders in the club and had secured investment from Hong Kong and elsewhere. This injection of cash allowed manager Steve Evans, no stranger to financial controversy himself, to recruit some of the highest-rated players at this level. Over a six-month period, twenty-three players came in, notably Tubbs at £55,000 from Salisbury, Torres at £100,000 from Peterborough, and Brodie, for a new Conference record of £275,000, from York.

Members of Crawley's tiny fan base were rubbing their eyes in disbelief. The club was in administration in the late 1990s, and again in 2006. There was a campaign to get shot of previous owners when the club was around £1.1 million in debt, a hefty chunk owed to HMRC. Somehow the club struggled through this, and then survived a winding-up order. The new investments completely turned things around with the local council chipping in by leasing the impressive little Broadfield Stadium to the club. Inevitably, opposition fans had nurtured a righteous disdain for a club that seemed to be buying its way to success. Crawley were already being dismissed as 'the Manchester City of the Conference'. Add to this the outspoken antics of manager Evans, and you could be sure few now recognised Crawley as romantic underdogs any more. They'd lost on the season's opening day but hadn't looked back since, hitting top spot in September.

A crowd of just 1,412 cheered Crawley to first place, but nearly five times that number roll up at Kenilworth Road on the last Tuesday of September to see if Luton could close the gap. Free-scoring Mansfield were the visitors, second in the table and a good test for our inconsistent side. Just hours before kick-off came the news we'd signed Amari Morgan-Smith – at twenty-one, hailed as one of the hottest properties in non-League circles – and he went straight into the team. He enjoyed a lively scoring debut, but all the headlines focused on a new piece of Luton carnage for the history books: we contrived to miss three penalties in a passage of play lasting around 5 minutes.

During this crazy spell, there were also two players sent off. A good contest had reached boiling point shortly before the interval, when Mills handled and Gnakpa's resultant penalty was saved. The ref immediately ordered a retake, and Crow stepped up to see his effort also saved. As everybody piled towards the rebound near the byeline, a huge melee ensued, leading to Stags captain Foster and manager Holdsworth being red carded. As the dugouts were positioned in front of hospitality boxes, the furious Holdsworth couldn't simply disappear into the stands, but had to make a 100-yard walk of shame, hot on the heels of his captain.

There was no sign of any cooling off during the interval, for within a minute of the restart, Luton were given a third chance from the spot, this time Barnes-Homer skying an awful effort high over the bar. Excitement levels remained high and Crow made amends 5 minutes later, thrashing an angled shot into the net. Three minutes further on, and debutant Morgan-Smith volleyed in a rebound to seal the three points. A perfect end to a whirlwind day for the new boy, who was wearing electric blue boots he'd bought in Luton town centre just hours before kick-off. A month that began mired in gloom for LTFC thus ended on a real high.

October 2010: Winding Up the Sensitive Kid

Big summer signing Adam Murray had joined rivals Mansfield after just half a dozen games. The boss made a quick decision there. It was a surprise and brought back memories of quick U-turns by previous Town managers. I recall Steve Claridge, Steve Elliott and Andy Harrow, major signings during separate summers, being moved on by David Pleat surprisingly quickly. But the fastest exit of all must have been Scotland international Robbie Winters, who arrived in 2002 from Aberdeen. He was hauled off at half-time on his debut by Joe Kinnear and invited to continue his career elsewhere. Kinnear was never one to dither; after bringing Tresor Kandol on as a sub at Notts County in 2001, he dragged him off again after just a few minutes.

Town crept into fourth place by winning 1-0 at Barrow for the second successive campaign, the first-half domination topped off by Barnes-Homer arrowing home a low drive. The second period saw narrow escapes as Barrow battled hard, but it proved a happy trek home for 228 heroic fans. There were only a couple of days to recover before the stiffest home test so far, leaders Crawley bringing their expensively assembled squad to perform under Tuesday night lights.

In a see-saw contest, in-form Drury ended our penalty hoodoo by firing us ahead after a foul on Kroca. A second goal looked essential to keep dangerous visitors at bay, but it never came and nemesis Brodie levelled things after our defence switched off at a short corner. Crawley pushed forward boldly and left space at the back, but Crow wasted a golden chance and a Barnes-Homer lob missed by inches. Sickeningly, we went down in the very last minute, Wright squaring for McAllister to slot a smash-and-grab winner. It was hard to stomach, and the players looked stunned as they trooped off.

Money reacted by bemoaning the toughest early-season fixture list that anyone in this division had to face, but at least he had an eleven-day break to try and raise spirits again. It was then off to the seaside at Eastbourne for the next 90-minute adventure. Pilkington headed us into an early lead before we were pegged back against the run of play by Cook's goal. Four goals arrived in the final 27 minutes, ultimately leaving us smiling in the sunshine. A neat lob by Barnes-Homer was cancelled out by Johnson's close-range equaliser, but Crow bagged a brace for 4-2, his second from the spot.

Forest Green were having a hard time of it near the foot of the table, and Luton knew they must be beaten at Kenilworth Road if the promotion challenge was to stay on track. A potential banana skin? We needn't have worried for it was one-way traffic and chances galore were created, half a dozen of them billowing the net behind the overworked Bittner. Morgan-Smith was beginning to look a great signing, revelling in a left-sided attacking role, with Crow looking confident too. They bagged three between them, Drury and Barnes-Homer also on target. The night was capped by a brilliant first career goal for Walker, his 25-yard rocket coming in the dying seconds. The ground erupted, but Walker looked mysteriously nonchalant, later admitting he was actually frozen with excitement and had no idea how to celebrate!

Neighbours St Albans City, who toiled away a division below us, didn't pose too many problems four days later in the fourth qualifying round of the FA Cup. A classy hat-trick by Morgan-Smith and a goal from Crow did the necessary. Nobody was really complaining about 4-0, even though Money apologised for spells in the game where we looked a little sloppy. With more than 60 per cent of possession and twenty-two shots on goal, few really noticed.

The visit of newly promoted Bath City at the tail-end of October coincided with LTFC's 125th anniversary weekend. Those pink-and-blue club colours from 1885 were regenerated and worn again today, a number of former players paraded around the pitch and a bumper match programme was published. We were treated to some great memories and reminded what an amazing history our little club had. Chairman Nick Owen told how his late father started coming here after returning from Second World War hostilities; MD Gary Sweet revealed he was ballboy for the 1975 visit of Chelsea, and recalled the occasion he was sent out of the house to buy a packet of fags for his dad but ended up travelling to an away game at Sunderland instead.

It would have been impertinent of the current players not to turn on the style amid such nostalgia and celebration, and fortunately they were in the right mood to do so against opposition posing very little threat. An opportunist early goal by Crow that left the 'keeper injured got things underway, with Pilkington and Atieno strikes completing a routine 3-1 victory. We were up to third, just three points adrift of Crawley. As well as the birthday party, the fixture also marked exactly a year in charge for Money. Although his record on paper looked reasonably good (twenty-six wins, nine draws, eleven losses – eighty-seven points gained) the jury was still out among fans over his capabilities. This uneasy situation was perfectly encapsulated by an episode in the Bath game after he sent Walker on as sub to liven things up, some fans reacting badly when he called off Crow and not Barnes-Homer.

Blogger David Mosque had the following to say:

> We witnessed one of the most cringeworthy responses to a substitution I can recall for many a year. I watched Money's reactions throughout. He was livid initially with the booing and reacted, and then went into a mega-huff when chanting started. He's a sensitive type. And we all learnt at school how to wind up the sensitive kid. He has a strange and spiky relationship with the fans. I think he has to understand that he is in a relationship with damaged goods: a fandom who have been through hell and back, and he is expecting everyone, even the dimwits who would boo their own players, to react to his decisions rationally.

November 2010: Back to the Valley of Normality

Luton's so-called reward for booting St Albans out of the FA Cup was a first-round tie at the humble Rockingham Triangle athletics stadium, home of Corby Town. Bad memories flooded back for older fans who recalled being 'giant-killed' by this mob in the 1960s, back when we were paid-up members of the ninety-two club. The modern Corby is no longer an ugly unemployment black spot and has the country's fastest growing population, but the prospect of a return visit was not particularly stimulating. Money rested three regulars, and the slightly weakened side gained a 1-1 draw at the Conference North club, Barnes-Homer's late header creeping across the line to cancel out an early goal by unmarked Mackey. Home 'keeper MacKenzie made fine saves and an unwanted replay became necessary.

It was an altogether different proposition – big ground, wide open spaces, experienced opposition – when we travelled to Wrexham on a Thursday evening for another live television match. Full-back Murray, soon to be given leave for a hernia operation, slipped in the opening minutes, allowing Mangan a simple goal. Battling a fierce wind, Town forced a dozen corners, but were repelled time and again, and slipped to a fifth defeat of the season. But there was soon good news off the field as we captured the signatures of three highly rated Conference performers: York midfielder Alex Lawless, Barrow striker Jason Walker and Newport winger Charlie Henry. All three were loan deals, but there was an agreement in advance that they would become permanent deals in the next transfer window. In addition, we borrowed Craig Hinton from Northampton as defensive cover. Other Conference clubs no doubt cast envious eyes at our ability to attract top names at this level, but Luton officials emphasised that they ran a tight ship, and these moves were only possible because of the exits of Gallen and Pilkington.

Just forty-eight hours after Wrexham, we travelled to face Altrincham, Money admitting he ignored his usual policy of taking pressure off players by telling them this was a must-win game. The Robins may have been bottom of the table, but seemed a resilient lot and held us at bay until early in the second half, new boy Lawless poking home a disputed goal from close range. A scruffy sort of win, but it saw us third in the table, just two points adrift of a lead being swapped week to week between Crawley and Wimbledon.

Luton were never in difficulty in the replay with Corby once Barnes-Homer fired his eleventh of the season in the opening minutes. Things went further downhill for the visitors when Jarman was red carded after a flurry of violent clashes with the Luton management team when he tried to retrieve the ball from their dugout with a little too much haste. Money's right-hand man Brabin featured prominently in the exchanges and he too was sent off, taking up residence in a hospitality box nearby. Atieno (2) and Gnakpa gave us a 4-0 lead, which could have been even bigger, and the margin allowed Money to push on three young subs, only to see Corby poach two late goals that gave the scoreline an unrealistic look. In round two, we were drawn to face Charlton at The Valley, which felt like a pleasant return to historical normality. It was a mouth-watering prospect, and I suspect I wasn't the only one to suddenly stop calling Cup games 'low priority.'

In the meantime, back to Conference action and Histon's visit was our fourth game in ten days. However, Cup commitments and bad weather were about to strike and this would prove our last 90 minutes of league action for six long weeks. The club from ye olde parish of Histon and Impington pitched up with a mere fifty-three fans, and were sent packing with a 5-1 trouncing that took us, albeit briefly, into second. This was a routine and comfortable win, with Walker heading a debut goal and Gnakpa showboating with the fans in typical fashion after a towering header from a corner. It was so stress-free that even Barnes-Homer was able to net a penalty. Drury and Atieno bagged the others, and we were now just a point off the top with nearly half the programme completed.

This healthy state of affairs, added to the looming Cup tie, lifted spirits considerably until a spell of bad weather came along and interrupted the momentum. November ended with major snowfalls, up to 30 cm in places, across most of Britain, some spots recording their coldest November nights on record. But in semi-frozen south-east London, Luton's Cup tie at The Valley soon made us forget the cold. We gave League One opposition a run for its money and enjoyed being free of the Conference pressures that weigh so heavily.

Charlton, forty-nine places above us, were on a long unbeaten run and took the lead when Anyinsah was left unmarked to head home. Barnes-Homer struck wood with a 30-yard screamer as Luton hit back. Then Morgan-Smith was tripped and Drury stepped forward to become the latest man to miss a Luton penalty, but he won instant redemption by stooping to head home the rebound off 'keeper Elliot. Jackson regained the home side's lead before the break, but Luton were far from finished. Drury's magical curling shot from 25 yards left Elliot flat-footed, and would prove one of the goals of the season. Penalty appeals were waved away when Gnakpa dramatically hit the deck, but, undaunted, we headed for home delighted to have earned a replay. Interesting how comfortable we looked in League One surroundings. After scrapping with the Histons and Corbys of this world, it was strangely comforting to be back in the type of environment we were more used to. Roll on the day of our return.

December 2010: Sophie's Choice Remarks

The earliest widespread snowfalls for seventeen winters led to Luton games at Wimbledon and Forest Green being called off, although the weather relented to allow the Charlton replay to proceed in front of live television cameras. A third-round tie away to Tottenham was the big fat carrot being dangled. Luton dominated, and after Crow and Keane went agonisingly close, Kroca strolled forward to smash home a loose ball after a corner. Wagstaff's near-post header levelled matters in Charlton's first meaningful attack, just before half-time. The party was well and truly pooped when a neat Anyinsah flick and Jackson's deflected free-kick beat Tyler late in the game to make it 1-3. Further bad news saw Crow, Morgan-Smith and Murray join Blackett and Newton on a lengthening injury list.

Inevitably, Money reshuffled the side to face Welling in the FA Trophy in a Sunday home tie that pulled in less than 2,000 and ended goalless. The hastily arranged replay two days later was watched by 404, thought to be the lowest crowd at a competitive first team match since we had visited the now-defunct Thames exactly eighty years earlier. Goals by Lawless and

Walker took us through 2-1, but interest was scant and, in view of the injury list, the trophy was being regarded as little more than an irritant.

A week before Christmas, more than 6,000 turned out in dreadful conditions for the visit of York. The referee deemed the pitch playable at 10 a.m., and 200 York fans made it in time for kick-off. Then heavy snow began to fall and after fifty-five slippery, goalless minutes, the contest was abandoned, both managers in full agreement with the decision. With the weather and road conditions deteriorating, the visiting fans experienced a nightmare journey home. York's spokeswoman Sophie Hicks was quoted later as blaming Luton for these problems rather than the weather, and called for financial compensation. Her comments didn't impress her counterparts at the Luton end, especially as she hadn't travelled down herself. It was pointed out that many home fans lived outside Bedfordshire and had had travel problems too.

Britain continued to shiver through and beyond the holiday period and the trip to Rushden and Diamonds and the home match with Tamworth were both duly frozen off. No football at Christmas – *quelle horreur*! It left six games to rearrange as we ended the calendar year in fourth place, albeit with three games in hand on others.

January 2011: Cerys' Post-Wedding Disappointment

On New Year's Day, Luton hosted Rushden and Diamonds, a club recently rocked by the sad news goalkeeper Dale Roberts, twenty-four, had taken his own life. The subsequent turmoil led to two games being postponed and the Luton game was their first action since the tragedy. As a mark of respect they 'retired' their No. 1 shirt. Some would recall Roberts from last season's game at Nene Park when he enjoyed some banter with Luton fans near the end of the 'dead rubber' contest in April. An inquest heard Roberts had struggled to come to terms with an injury, and with media coverage about his fiancée's relationship with a teammate. Further sad news broke at Kenilworth Road about the death of Terry Branston, who captained Luton to promotion back in 1968.

Rushden were comfortably seen off 3-0, Barnes-Homer producing two well-taken goals either side of half-time and Gnakpa's low drive sealing things. The latter repeated his trick of scoring 15 minutes from time just three days later, his deflected shot proving the game's only goal at Hayes and Yeading. It was a fourth successive league win, but only 801 were at the Church Road ground to see it – the smallest post-war crowd at any Luton league game. The winner came as blessed relief as it had begun to look as if the struggling West Londoners would nick another point to match their draw at our place in August.

The second of three away trips in nine days saw nineteen Luton shots on goal fail to bring success at Bath City's Twerton Park. The woodwork was smitten twice, and Gnakpa missed a glorious close-range opportunity with his head. Although languishing below halfway, the Romans posed plenty of problems and Town did well to keep another clean sheet. With the last kick of the game, Lawless smashed a shot against the bar, meaning us 965 foot soldiers departed frustrated, feeling two points had been dropped. The attractions of Bath's fine city centre provided some compensation. Especially disappointed not to see Luton score was singer Cerys Matthews, attending the game despite having married her agent Steve Abbott only twenty-four hours earlier. Steve, a big Hatters fan, admitted the wedding in Wales and their honeymoon in Africa had all been arranged to fit in with this Luton game. Cerys, lead singer with the band Catatonia, had been a committed Luton fan since the couple had been together.

It remained tight at the top, and we tackled leaders AFC Wimbledon at Kingsmeadow knowing a win would see us hit top spot on goal difference, leapfrogging the Dons and Crawley in the process. Like Luton, Terry Brown's upstarts had drawn their last two, and there was tension in the damp South London air on this night. After some nervy exchanges, both sides desperate not to make mistakes, Luton improved as the game went on, and we again rued a series of near misses. Walker and Man of the Match Drury both struck the woodwork. Another clean sheet away from home was good news, but on the other hand we'd now scored just once in nearly 300 minutes.

The chances were being created, but we clearly needed more cutting edge. Money moved to correct this with a short-term fix, agreeing a four-month contract with veteran Ghanaian striker Lloyd Owusu. He'd scored goals for seven league clubs, and at thirty-four had most recently been playing in Australia.

After further progress in the FA Trophy, when a youthful side cruised past Uxbridge to the tune of 4-0, York came to town for the important business and Owusu went straight into the team. No sign of any snow this time, and the pivotal moments came early when goalkeeper Ingham brought Gnakpa crashing down on the edge of his area after less than 15 minutes' action. Ingham was red carded and the visitors didn't have a goalkeeper on their bench. Skipper Chris Smith volunteered for the yellow jersey, but was immediately beaten by the resultant free-kick, hammered in by Drury.

Home fans were baying for the blood of bogey side York, for there would surely be no better opportunity to give them a tonking. Gnakpa duly headed the second, then debutant Owusu converted a corner at the near post. Owusu rolled out his distinctive goal celebration, rhythmically thrusting open-palmed hands skywards, which, we were told later, signified 'Raise the roof!' Luton fans liked the look of that one, and would soon be joining in. Just before half-time, big Kroca strolled forward to volley a fourth. Smith did his best between the sticks, and in the second half restricted Luton to just one additional goal to make it 5-0, sub Atieno heading home. The hapless visitors were reduced to nine men when Jonathan Smith collected a second yellow card.

Four days later, Gateshead were the visitors and a bizarre match encapsulated all that supporting Luton was about. Shockingly, we fell two behind after only 16 minutes, but turned the tables and clawed back the deficit (scorers Crow and Gnakpa). The Heed had a man sent off and we went in for the break all square and a man to the good. But instead of the expected surge to victory, the second period was 45 minutes of sheer frustration on a gluepot pitch. Gateshead changed their tactics after the red card, and we simply could not find a way through. The 6,000 crowd went home wondering how a team of such slender resources and ambition could take three points out of four from Luton in a single season. The nearest we got to a winner was sub Atieno's shot flying off target from close range – the very last kick of the game. It was Atieno's last contribution, for he would be among those released in a big exodus at the end of January.

Also departing was the Czech Besta, who never settled after that unhappy start in August, plus out-of-favour Gallen and youngster Nathaniel. No shocks there, but the bad news was the added departure of our most effective player that season, midfielder Drury, who joined Championship side Ipswich for £150,000, a clause in his contract meaning there was nothing the club could do to keep him once the offer came in. Not long ago, Drury was a part-timer who also worked as a bricklayer, but few players have made such an impact as he in such a short stint at Luton (twenty-three games). Ipswich were getting a twenty-seven-year-old late-starter who'd never played in the Football League, and Luton were losing a key man. The good news was that a chunk of the Drury cash was being invested in Cambridge's nippy young winger Robbie Willmott. Additionally, just minutes before the deadline, we grabbed Northampton defender Luke Graham. He was a real loan ranger, for we were the seventh club to have borrowed him in his eight-year career.

On the field, a hectic and unbeaten January (eight games in twenty-six days) drew to a close with the visit of Grimsby. An excellent first-half display climaxed with Gnakpa in acres of space to fire in a Lawless pass. The second goal, which would have allowed us all to relax, never came. As the second half dragged on, nails were bitten and blood pressure rose until the final whistle signalled vital points in the bag. It wasn't pretty, but we ended the month four points behind leaders Wimbledon with two games in hand.

February 2011: Seven in a Row at Home, Sweet Home

A combination of the quirky Conference fixture list, FA Trophy commitments and rearranged matches led to Luton playing seven successive matches at home in a twenty-eight-day period. During this spell, the stadium also hosted an England 'C' international. No wonder our groundsman wasn't fond of Februarys.

Worries over how we'd cope without the departed Drury were blown away when Darlington were buried 4-0. Patience was required as the game remained deadlocked at 0-0 until the 68th minute, but Gnakpa's 25-yarder then opened the floodgates and by the end everyone was jubilant. Owusu knocked in two well-taken efforts, and the rout was completed in the final minute by a classy Lawless goal that had the manager purring with delight. A lively cameo by debutant Willmott was another reason to be cheerful.

Good momentum had been achieved by the eleven-game unbeaten run at this point, and it seemed a shame the next fixture was a mere FA Trophy tie with no league points at stake. Gloucester City of the Conference North adopted a physical approach on a windy Friday night at a sparsely populated Kenilworth Road and a Luton reserve side scraped through to the quarter-finals with a late goal. Defender Graham was the unlikely hero, springing the offside trap and slotting home nicely.

Fellow promotion hopefuls Fleetwood made their first visit to Luton the following weekend, manager Micky Mellon saying some complimentary things about our style and philosophy. Worryingly, he also considered Kenilworth Road a lucky ground, having scored the first and last goals of his sixteen-year career here. Fleetwood were a club going places fast, thanks largely to major investment by the entrepreneurial Andy Pilley, founder of a power supply firm. Formed in 1997, they had only gone fully professional a few months ago, but already looked serious play-off contenders.

Those who scoffed at Money recruiting an ageing striker from Australia were eating their words. Owusu had hit the ground running and netted his fourth goal in five games to put us ahead against Fleetwood. But joy was short-lived, as within two minutes Seddon ghosted behind our defence to equalise. From here it was 80 minutes of pure frustration for Town fans, visiting defenders, officials and occasionally even our own players, all getting it in the neck. Early in the second half, well-taken goals by Taylor and Seddon punished us severely, and the Cod Army tactics kept us at bay. Lawless hit the bar with a pile driver, but generally this was a below-par Luton.

Money was not happy with a lack of solidity and leadership in midfield, and took experienced campaigner Paul Carden on loan from Cambridge, giving him his debut hours later in the Friday night clash at Newport. Carden combined with Keane to tee up Willmott, who slipped Town into the lead from the far post after 18 minutes. Reformed from the ashes of the old Newport County, this evening's hosts were, like Fleetwood, playing at this level for the first time and desperate to take the scalp of Luton Town. We hung on to our slim lead grimly, and when Tyler made a brilliant save with 93 minutes on the clock, it looked as if we'd done enough. The fourth official had indicated four minutes of additional time, but 95 minutes had passed when one last desperate home surge saw Carden impede Hatswell, a penalty was given and Collins kept his nerve to square the match. The M4 carried home 424 Hatters in a grumpy mood.

The month ended with a single-goal victory at Conference North newcomers Guiseley, to win a place in the FA Trophy semi-finals. Barnes-Homer raced clear to neatly lift a shot over the 'keeper. However, this week there weren't too many smiling faces around Kenilworth Road, for our chances of automatic promotion appeared to be drifting away on the February wind. We remained third, but were now twelve points behind leaders Wimbledon, having played a massive five games fewer, but, more significantly, second-placed Crawley were nine points better off than Luton, and had played a game less. It was the Sussex side who were hot favourites for the title, Steve Evans' men having enjoyed a fabulous winter, unbeaten in the league since mid-October. Even a run to the fifth round of the FA Cup – where they went out narrowly at Manchester United – hadn't harmed their league prospects.

March 2011: Break-Up of a Spiky Relationship

There were plenty of points still to play for as spring threatened to break out, but most Luton fans were long-suffering realists and had accepted by now that we'd be settling for play-offs again this season. Despite this, overall expectation levels remained sky-high, and it was clearly going to take more than a couple of good wins over York and Darlington to lift the mood for any length of time. Most games felt like a real struggle, full of tension and frustration. It appeared to stem from the way lesser opponents were inspired to raise their game against us, working feverishly to disrupt and stifle. True class and skill is uncommon in this league, but that doesn't make it easy to get out of. Nevertheless, home crowds were holding up well, by far the highest outside the League at an average of 6,376.

It would need a lengthy winning run to challenge Crawley now, and although March began with three points from a trip to Forest Green, it proved another nervy, scrappy affair on a chilly Tuesday night. The New Lawn pitch was sandy and the wind fierce in the Gloucestershire hills, but we were never in serious trouble once Owusu poked the ball under goalkeeper Bittner. No-nonsense Carden was introduced with half an hour left to ensure we kept what we'd got. It wasn't pretty, but it was three points won.

We'd now hit the final third of the season and couldn't afford any slips in the remaining seven home games, with Kidderminster's visit the first of these. We looked positive enough; Owusu was booked for diving after just 20 seconds and then went close with a low shot. Barnes-Homer seemed highly motivated against his old pals, and gave us the lead with a fierce shot from an angle, which crossed the line and came out again, requiring a conflab between officials before a goal was awarded. In-form Kiddy equalised with a far-post header after the interval, and then managed to repel all our desperate attempts to find a winner.

Knowing that, barring miracles, we'd almost certainly finish between second and fifth created a strange sort of limbo at Luton at this point. A sort of damage limitation mentality eroded the urgency and motivation that comes with needing to win games. Consolidation became the name of the game. Now is that pragmatism or lack of ambition? Depends if you're a manager or a fan, I suppose. In an interview with BBC local radio, Money again referred to what he called unacceptable comments and negativity towards him and the team by frustrated fans. He was correct that some of the barracking had been over the top, but his attitude begs the question whether he truly understood the deep-seated frustration and angst caused by our predicament. As one long-standing supporter pointed out, the actions, conduct and anger of Luton fans were magnified, enhanced and intensified by the fact we were supporting a team marooned in non-League because of the actions of external forces. It felt like we fans were shop floor workers out of a job because the directors gambled away the profits and the taxman closed the factory down – not because we weren't working hard enough or putting in enough effort.

Three days after failing to overcome Kiddy, Tamworth came to town, and we had visions of repeating the thrashing of York when they lost their goalkeeper to injury early on and had no replacement on the bench. Centre-back Marshall went into goal, and his pals rolled up their sleeves and defended deep to protect him. For half an hour or so all attempts to expose his frailties were unsuccessful and the tension grew, the boil finally lanced when Owusu headed home Howells' free-kick. On the hour the points were made safe as Barnes-Homer clouted home the second.

What we could probably have done without at this point was a two-legged FA Trophy semi-final with Mansfield – but at least it would be good practice for the play-off format. At Field Mill on a Sunday afternoon, Mitchley blasted the only goal to win the first leg for The Stags, but the home side's real hero was 'keeper Grof, who continually kept Luton at bay.

The second leg was just six days later, but before then we had to travel to Cambridge with league points at stake. This ended goalless, former U's favourite Willmott going closest when smashing a free-kick against the bar. Loanee Carden lined up again for Luton, despite technically still being assistant manager of the night's opponents. When he was substituted, the reaction of some Luton fans made it abundantly clear he was not proving a popular addition to our squad.

All in all, we didn't look like a team heading for the play-offs in a winning frame of mind. Money told fans in his programme notes there was no need to panic over this, but in the same publication, MD Sweet was less circumspect and admitted, 'The team is underperforming.'

Despite failure to score in more than 200 minutes of playing time, the possibility of reaching a Wembley Cup final helped pull in over 6,000 for the second leg against Mansfield. This competition lacked the cachet of our previous Wembley occasions, but having got this far, the cynics (this writer included) were being won over. Perhaps it was something to do with the fact there was no pressure to get league points, but that day – via some kind of mysterious, unspoken consensus – the Luton fans decided to eliminate all grumbling and turn the support volume up to max. This unexpected surge of enthusiasm spread around the stadium like wildfire and the backing was truly remarkable throughout, the mood inevitably spreading to the pitch. Owusu smashed Town ahead 50 seconds into the second half, and moments later narrowly missed a great chance to double the lead. But with extra time looming, Gnakpa picked up his second caution and departed, followed off within 5 minutes by Lawless for a bad challenge on Nix.

Facing 30 minutes of extra time with just nine men only galvanised the crowd further, and every tackle and every clearance got roars of approval. It looked like we'd done enough to earn a penalty shoot-out, but in the 118th minute the referee shocked everyone by spotting a handball and awarding the Stags a penalty. Mansfield players had been appealing for a corner and couldn't believe their luck. Briscoe's kick was well saved by Pilkington, but the rebound fell kindly and was scrambled home. Mansfield had made it to Wembley on a 2-1 aggregate. As Luton players sank to the turf in despair and fatigue, some of us pondered over why this sort of passion and commitment rarely seemed evident in league games.

It seemed a bit late in the day to be saying 'concentrate on the league', but a 1-0 win at Rushden and Diamonds three days later soon raised spirits again. The home club were struggling with major problems behind the scenes, and a magnificent Luton turnout of 1,227 travelling fans, exactly half the overall gate, expected nothing short of victory this night. A poor back pass by Huke in the early stages was pounced upon and netted by Willmott. Top defending ensured the lead was preserved. We were by now comfortably clear of the pack immediately outside the play-off zone, but Crawley's winning run remained relentless, meaning top place was well out of reach.

Remarkably, the club then raked in a six-figure fee for a player who'd never made a league appearance. After three years at the club's Centre of Excellence, sixteen-year-old Cauley Woodrow departed to Fulham, having recently become the first player in thirty-six years to represent England while on the books of a non-League club. It was another feather in our youth development cap, and the fee could rise further depending on various clauses in the deal. All this cash flying around was little consolation to the hundreds of Luton fans fearing imminent redundancy from the local Vauxhall plant, which had been facing closure after 100 years. Subsequently, General Motors decided against closure and jobs were saved.

With spring upon us, Luton's last lingering hopes of automatic promotion rested upon a major collapse by Crawley and victory by the Hatters in at least nine of their final dozen games. What we definitely didn't need at this point was a miserable, below-par performance at relegation-threatened Southport. But that's precisely what occurred, and the fallout proved cataclysmic. A poor first half at Haig Avenue ended goalless, and the game deteriorated further after the break. There was brief respite as Barnes-Homer netted against the run of play, but then despair as the home side responded with two goals in the final 8 minutes, both scorers left completely unattended to do their dirty deeds. A shocking end to a dismal display. Around 700 Luton fans made the round trip of nearly 400 miles and deserved better than this; one fan who'd missed very few games over the past forty-four years, Alan Adair, declared it the 'worst I have ever seen in my life – truly an atrocious effort'.

By all accounts, the MD and the manager began urgent discussions soon after the game, and continued these talks over the rest of the weekend. The outcome was a statement issued on the Monday that Richard Money had gone. He left by 'genuine mutual consent' said the club, a phrase that I suppose at least confirmed the widely held view that 'mutual consent' departures were rarely that at all! The parting of the ways was evidently unplanned, for only ten days earlier Gary Sweet had emphatically stated in the programme that any fans wanting a change of manager at this late stage of the season would be disappointed.

Money had a spiky relationship with fans throughout his eighteen months in charge, and was accused of constantly tinkering with line-ups and tactics. His overall track record showed he was an experienced and accomplished coach, but for Luton to be sitting fifteen points behind the league leaders after two seasons at this level was simply unacceptable. Added to all this, a ready-made replacement was waiting in the wings in the shape of his assistant Gary Brabin, a man who steered Cambridge to the 2009 Conference play-off final. Ironically, Money departed with the best record of any permanent manager in Luton history, having won forty-five and drawn twenty-one of his eighty-three games in charge. His exit was dignified and he talked well of the club as he left, a far cry from some of the earlier spats, including the time he warned fans calling for a new manager to be careful what they wished for. The choice of Brabin as successor wasn't greeted with universal approval, but was probably the safest option at this point of the season. Brabin's CV included playing for Hull and Blackpool, plus work as a nightclub bouncer, as well as non-League management.

The crowded fixture list meant Big Gary only had a matter of hours before sampling match-day action in full charge of things. Barrow were the Tuesday night visitors, languishing near the foot of the table and just the sort of opposition likely to upset our apple cart. Sure enough, as happened with Money, the home debut of a new manager proved a big anti-climax. Barrow sneaked off with a goalless draw, their energy and commitment a match for our rather nervy attempts to string a few passes together. It was the seventh time this season we'd failed to win a home match, but the grumbling in the aftermath was soon overshadowed by the awful news that devoted supporter and BBC broadcaster Ian Pearce had collapsed and died at his home shortly before the game. The alarm was only raised when he failed to show in the press box at kick-off time. Popular Pearcey was just fifty-six.

April 2011: The Great 'Guard of Honour' Mystery

It was all fun and games at Kidderminster, where four goals in a hectic last 10 minutes capped an end-to-end thriller, but Luton's reward was only a single point. Willmott curled in a handsome free-kick to cancel out McPhee's first-half penalty, then with the clock ticking down, Gnakpa conjured a very special goal, cutting in from the byeline and blasting home. Morris headed the home side level again, but Walker's low shot in the 90th minute put Town 3-2 up. Wild celebrations were cut rudely short in the 92nd minute when full-back Williams popped up to net a close-range equaliser.

A more adventurous approach became evident after Brabin's elevation, but his third game in charge ended with another frustrating finish, Kettering equalising in the last minute at Kenilworth Road for 2-2. The dreadful Southport debacle seemed to be out of Luton's system, but conceding late goals was becoming a nasty habit. A neat effort by Howells had been cancelled out by Solkhon dancing round 'keeper Tyler for 1-1, before Morgan-Smith converted a Howells cross. Mills pounced to equalise in additional time and another two points went astray.

The first win for Brabin was the return game with his former club Southport, a canter at 6-0, which came on the same day Crawley gained the points required to clinch the Conference title with five games left. Again the key action came late in the day, four of the goals hitting hapless Southport's net in the final 6 minutes. Morgan-Smith's free-kick and Willmott gained the crucial first-half lead, and the relegation-threatened visitors were humbled by Murray's first goal for the club and strikes by Walker, Kroca and a Gnakpa penalty in the dying moments.

In the wake of this handsome win, there was much, somewhat mischievous, media talk over whether or not Luton would form a guard of honour to welcome the new champions to the pitch when we travelled to Crawley three days later. Home boss Steve Evans seemed to think it was our duty to perform such a ritual, but Luton evidently disagreed, the teams walking out side by side as usual. We were sent reeling by a horrific start when our old friend Brodie netted after barely 30 seconds. Lawless subsequently poked home an equaliser and we matched the home side blow for blow during the rest of the game, which ended 1-1. Yet another draw followed, this one goalless at Mansfield, underlining how we were playing reasonably well going into the play-offs, dictating large passages of play, but not killing off opposition.

The first defeat under Brabin's command came by a single goal on a stormy night at York, who were making a late charge for the play-offs themselves. The main talking point was a flare-up in the first half after a dreadful late tackle on Keane by York's Kerr. Brabin remonstrated with the home bench, and the fracas led to him being red carded, and then manhandled away down the tunnel by stewards. He would later face police charges over all this, ultimately being fined by magistrates for threatening behaviour, but cleared of assault.

When the dust settled, Luton found they needed just a point from the final three games to be certain of a play-off berth. It was duly earned in a straightforward 3-0 beating of already-relegated Eastbourne at Kenilworth Road. We knocked the ball around nicely in the sunshine and confidence appeared high for the big task ahead. A fine Willmott double and a Gnakpa header found the target. There was more of the same at Histon two days later on Easter Monday, as our bottom-of-the-table hosts were crushed 4-0 at the Glassworld Stadium in a real stroll in the sun – Morgan-Smith, Barnes-Homer (2) and Gnakpa the scorers. The opposition again had little to play for, and were swept aside in highly encouraging fashion.

With Luton and Wrexham certain to finish third and fourth in the table respectively, we now knew the two would face each other in the two-legged play-off semi-final. Before then, they would be in opposition for the final (and least meaningful) game of the regular campaign. It ended all square at 1-1 thanks to Walker netting a late equaliser from the spot. Brabin had lost just one of his ten matches in charge thus far, and home fans were encouraged by much of what had happened since the change of manager five weeks earlier. There was an air of cautious optimism as the traditional lap of honour took place after the final whistle.

May 2011: Cocky Spot-Kick Goes Horribly Wrong

So, we were into the play-offs for a second successive season. Having cagily weighed each other up at Kenilworth Road five days earlier, Luton and Wrexham met again at the Racecourse for the real business. The clubs finished three points apart in the final table and had similar recent form. Looking for omens, we were cheered to find out Wrexham manager Dean Saunders, in his long and distinguished career, had been relegated eight times and never promoted. However, Saunders deserved enormous credit for hanging in there at troubled Wrexham for three years before steering them to their present position. As they were cementing their play-off place recently, ownership of the club dominated local headlines in North Wales. Potential purchasers in the frame had been named as a supporters' trust group, a transsexual local businesswoman, and former player Ashley Ward. A winding-up order was issued over an unpaid tax bill meaning, for once, it wasn't Luton's off-field troubles grabbing the headlines.

But we were in no mood to be overshadowed on the field, and a brilliant first-half performance meant the outcome was very nearly decided with three quarters of the tie still to play. A wonder goal by Lawless on 15 minutes got the party underway, the Welshman advancing from his own half to hammer a magnificent shot into the corner. Town were on the rampage and minutes later, Howells crashed a shot against the bar and then Keane missed when he went one-on-one with the 'keeper. The dominance paid off when Gnakpa received the ball in the corner of the area and smashed a spectacular second goal. Incredibly, the dream start got even better as a corner found Asafu-Adjaye on the edge of the box and his raking drive arrowed into the net. It was the young full-back's first goal in his sixty-seventh game.

Three-up in 35 minutes and fans were dreaming of the promised land. Brabin's attacking formation had paid dividends in a big way, and after the break the defence held firm. We almost added a fourth when Kroca hit a post and Keane went close in a grandstand finish. What great timing to produce the best display of the season; 3-0 up at halfway meant we had a foot in the Manchester final already. Kenilworth Road was packed to the gills for the second leg, and the natives were in party mood. Interviewed before kick-off by local radio, I told the presenter the only way we could be knocked out of our stride would be to make a bad start by maybe conceding an early goal or a silly penalty or suchlike. After 20 minutes' action I wish I'd kept my mouth shut, for that's exactly what occurred.

With less than 8 minutes gone, Mangan scored at the far post and 12 minutes later the ball struck Gleeson's left arm to give rejuvenated Wrexham a penalty. They could now reduce the deficit to just one goal with 70 minutes left, meaning the next few seconds could be pivotal in respect of the outcome for an entire season's work. The experienced Taylor stepped up and arrowed the ball towards the corner, but Tyler made a brilliant save down to his left, the ball squirming away from him and hitting a post before he swooped on it a second time. Tyler pointed jubilantly to somebody in the upper main stand as Luton fans raised the roof in celebration. If there has ever been a louder roar for something other than a goal, I've yet to hear it.

This moment of drama going in our favour created a sense that the mini crisis was over. This would be our day. Sure enough, 8 minutes later, 'keeper Maxwell came off his line for a free-kick and Kroca looped a header over him. The aggregate lead was back to three and there'd be no looking back now. Ten minutes from time, Walker forced home Gnakpa's cross, and at 5-1 it really was game over. The following evening AFC Wimbledon had a surprisingly comfortable ride against Fleetwood to join us in the final. Promotion back to the league was now a mere 90 minutes away.

The final was set for Saturday 21 May at the home of big-spending Manchester City, not particularly convenient for two clubs and their fans based in the South East of the country. The ticket price of £41 (plus compulsory booking fee and postage) seemed extortionate to many for a game between non-League clubs. Mind you, we'd suffered two seasons of Conference 'inconvenience' by now, so more of the same was no surprise. The crowd subsequently numbered 18,195, two thirds of whom were backing Luton, and it was clear a hefty number from both clubs had been forced to stay away because of the prohibitive costs, especially those in family groups. A final at Wembley or any other London ground, combined with sensible pricing, would surely have seen a crowd nearer 30,000? After all, there were 40,000 Luton fans at Wembley for the JPT final just two years ago.

Even more inconvenient, however, was the strange story from the USA that received wide media coverage, about an evangelist broadcaster announcing the end of the world would occur at 1800 hours on 21 May. As our kick-off was 1500, it meant we would just get enough time for a penalty shoot-out if needed. If we were to miss promotion via penalties it would feel like the end of the world anyway.

As social media would later reveal, I wasn't the only one at the game who thought the pre-match opera singers and other USA-style nonsense was unnecessary. Fireworks in bright sunshine? The national anthem? What was that all about? Why were we dumbing down football? If it was to attract more youngsters and families to the game then reducing costs might have been a better answer. Surely such trimmings, if necessary at all, should have been saved for the FA Cup final and internationals?

The game was tense and poised on a knife-edge throughout. Wimbledon were physical and energetic just like their predecessor club, and Luton were showing flashes of attractive football in a new kit being introduced early for next season. It was a version of the orange shirt with white vertical stripes that was popular in the mid-seventies, worn during our second spell in football's top flight. With so much at stake, the contest remained deadlocked, and all the key moments occurred at the tail-end of proceedings. First a slide-rule pass found Walker, who was confronted by onrushing 'keeper Brown, but Walker touched the ball past him only for his legs to be whipped away. Remarkably, the twenty-seven-year-old PE teacher in charge took no action. Cue disbelief all round, including in the neutral television commentary box where even our old friend Steve Evans, Crawley manager, called it 'a stonewall penalty'. A minute later, the injustice was compounded in an incident in which the laws of geometry were tested. What shape could Manchester City's posts be? Normally, when a ball hits the inside of an upright from a 45-degree angle, it rebounds into the net and not back out in the same direction. But that's precisely what happened when Walker got on the end of a fine Howells cross with his head, squeezing his way between two taller defenders. As he hit the ground, Walker couldn't see where the ball had gone, and when he realised it was in the 'keeper's hands, his bemused and frozen facial expression told the story. How did that happen?

Into extra time we went and still nobody could score. The final whistle signalled a shoot-out and it dawned on us that we had now played 300 minutes of football with AFC Wimbledon this season and they had not managed a single goal against us in three matches plus extra-time. Surely we weren't about to lose to them now? Things continued to go against us. The penalty shoot-out was staged entirely at the opposite end to the Luton supporters, and we were not able to call upon Crow, one of our best finishers, as the attempt to bring him on as a late sub somehow failed amid the general mayhem of the dying moments.

Promotion hinged on the subsequent few minutes, and many could not bear to look. For the neutral there was romance in whoever succeeded: Wimbledon were a club built by their fans from the ashes of a miserable franchising operation, promoted six times from lower leagues in the past nine years to get here; Luton's backstory was all about bouncing back from mismanagement and harsh points deductions that punished fans and players instead of the guilty parties.

The build-up to the shoot-out involved the usual endless milling around by players, coaches and other hangers-on, and served to crank up the unbearable tension further. Wimbledon's goalkeeper appeared to be studying a scrap of paper, which was presumably a crib sheet on how Luton players took penalties. Was this allowed? Or, more to the point, was it going to be useful? We watched Luton every week and never knew who would take the next penalty, never mind where it would go. Finally, with the end of the world looming (allegedly) in 15 minutes, Lawless stepped up first. His body language was not looking the most positive, and he steered an unconvincing shot toward the left corner, but Brown guessed correctly and parried it (0-0). Hatton went for a similar area but applied more height and power (0-1). Pilkington then calmly lifted his shot into the roof of the net to Brown's left (1-1). Moore produced a carbon copy of Pilkington's (1-2). Newton looked assured and clinically fired the ball left, sending Brown the wrong way (2-2). Mohamed was Wimbledon's first failure, his weak low effort saved by Tyler's legs (2-2). We breathed again – all square after three attempts each.

Walker, unlucky victim of the two incidents at the end of normal time, stepped forward and to everyone's astonishment tried a 'Panenka dink' (for the uninitiated, a disguised and languid chip to the middle of the goal). It was high-risk and only attempted by the supremely skilful, supremely confident or supremely daft. Even Gary Lineker and Peter Crouch have come a cropper with this method in the past. For Walker it also went horribly wrong, his chip was gentle enough to give the diving Brown time to stretch an arm back where he came from to paw it away (2-2). We could be sure that one wasn't on Brown's crib sheet, for Walker's penalty in the semi-final had been low, hard and perfectly placed. Luton fans couldn't believe what they'd just witnessed.

Yakubu stepped up and his effort looked casual and unconvincing too, but as Tyler had dived the wrong way it drifted into the net (2-3). Howells was next, knowing a miss would see Luton beaten, but he responded with a beauty into the top corner to Brown's left (3-3). In characteristic 'no middle ground' fashion, Luton had conjured up three brilliant penalties and two awful ones. The onus was now on Wimbledon's leading marksman Kedwell to net the tenth penalty and put them in the Football League. Brabin stood motionless and barely blinking, but his opposite number Terry Brown looked a nervous wreck, wobbling around and striking up brief conversations with nearby policemen. Kedwell looked focused and highly motivated and steamed up to the ball, smashing it home to Tyler's right, both feet leaving the ground as he struck it.

One end of the stadium went bananas, the other was a picture of abject misery. Lutonians sank into their seats, head in hands, some screaming profanities, some standing silent and motionless, some making for the exit, others having no idea where to run or what to do. AFC Wimbledon achieving league status against the odds so soon after formation was a wonderful football story, but that was of little consolation to the people dressed in orange. How could promotion to the Football League rest on such small margins? Had one young man not decided to try something different when the world was watching him, this could have been us celebrating; Walker sat near the halfway line in floods of tears, and it was he who inevitably felt the wrath of fans who needed somebody or something to blame. Lawless also missed, but at least his effort was seen as conventional and worthy. Had Walker succeeded with his 'dink', of course we would be hailing him a genius, the new Lionel Messi. Such is football.

In the wake of the Manchester disaster, Brabin was awarded a two-year contract extension as a reward for Luton's brighter football of late, but the departures included Kroca, Gnakpa, Newton and Owusu and – significantly – the sad figure of Walker, who signed for York, his parting shot being something about being unable to settle in the south of England. You got the feeling this was a wise move, as Luton fans can be unforgiving and his life might not have been made easy had he stayed.

It was sickening to be contemplating a third season in non-League hell. Who would have predicted this a few years ago? Instead of the likes of Plymouth, Swindon and Bradford City next season, we would instead be doing battle with Braintree, Telford and Alfreton...

3

2011/12 Season

August 2011: One Rule for the Rich...

Preparing for this unexpected third tilt at getting out of the Conference, it felt like a good time to take stock. We'd now missed the boat in two play-off sagas, one of them desperately narrowly; we were on our third manager since exiting the league; and the sense of injustice at merely being here was still burning strongly and was showing no sign of disappearing.

The latter was hardly helped by a recent episode at QPR, crowned winners of the Championship in May. Regarded as stinking rich due to the personal wealth of their owners, Rangers incurred a fine (nothing else folks, just a fine) for misdemeanours surrounding the signing of Argentine midfielder Alejandro Faulin, a regular in the team throughout the last season. He joined for a reported club record £3.5 million, but it transpired he was sold to Rangers by an agency and not a club, and was joining them effectively on a 'Bosman'. The FA got involved because of potential 'third party ownership' offences and Rangers looked to be in big trouble. They were duly found guilty of seeking to pay an unauthorised agent as part of the deal – the same offence for which Luton's previous owners were found guilty and severely punished with deducted points. As our MD Gary Sweet pointed out, that punishment relegated Luton and cost the club more than £2 million in costs and loss of revenue, not to mention the organic football progression we would have expected otherwise. It was a far cry from the penalty QPR had just received – they merely had to cough up a six-figure fine, and their promotion to the Premiership was left unaffected, which would easily generate the income to cover the fine. Double standards or what?

Amid the euphoria and high hopes of a new campaign getting underway in August sunshine, some of Luton's misery at being stuck in non-League hell was moderated by positive noises from the club about the future. We were assured that since the 2007 crisis that led to LTFC 2020's takeover, stability had been achieved, legal battles fought, massive debts paid off, huge losses and books balanced, relationships repaired and basic business systems introduced. If anyone was in any doubt over the importance of all this, they only had to cast an eye up the road to Rushden and Diamonds, in the Football League six years ago, who had now been expelled from the Conference and placed in administration.

Oddly, our third season at this level got underway with a strange and unique event – a blank opening Saturday. The game at newly promoted AFC Telford was postponed due to stretched police resources in the wake of recent urban riots, some of which were in the West Midlands, on the day of a planned English Defence League march in Telford itself. It meant our first game would now be the visit of Forest Green Rovers on a Tuesday night.

Green energy tycoon Dale Vince is in command of FGR these days. Following his ban on red meat, installation of solar panels, and introduction of the world's first organic football pitch, hopes were high his club would put in a serious promotion challenge. But whatever the new expectation levels at Forest Green, they would not match the pressures here at Kenilworth Road. Brabin unveiled five new Hatters signings for full debuts – Curtis Osano, Will Antwi, Dean Beckwith, Aaron O'Connor and James Dance – but despite dominating possession, Luton failed to bury chances and a Beckwith headed equaliser was all we had to cheer in a 1-1 draw.

The clear lack of cutting edge prompted urgent Luton cash bids for Forest Green's Styche and Gateshead's Shaw, but both were knocked back. The following Saturday the smiles returned, albeit late in the day. Southport scored early at Kenilworth Road, and a poor first half was only saved when youngster Watkins levelled from distance just before the break. Southport prolonged the agony until Askrigg was sent off for a second caution, prompting an opening of the floodgates. Four goals arrived in a late 7-minute segment, well-taken efforts by Antwi, Morgan-Smith, Willmott and Crow.

Three days later came one of the trickiest contests of the season, Mansfield away. It ended all square, Antwi bagging another to cancel out Green's smart first-half strike. By contrast, Braintree Town came to town four days later, the little Essex club enjoying their first month in the heady heights of English football's fifth-tier. They had flattened Grimsby 5-0 less than a fortnight ago, but at Luton were humbled 3-1, all the goals coming in the first period – two from Morgan-Smith, including the rebound from a saved penalty, and one by Howells.

Those Luton penalty jitters continued at the end of the month at Hayes and Yeading. Soares stole in to put the underdogs ahead after just 4 minutes, before two Luton spot-kicks were saved, Crow and Howells the guilty parties. The latter's effort was pushed out to the feet of Morgan-Smith, who slid it home to roars of great relief. Moments later, Crow was able to atone and put Town in front. The joy was short-lived, for Soares popped up again to punish slack defending on the stroke of half-time. It ended 2-2 and felt like two points frittered away, even though we remained unbeaten in August.

Seven first-teamers on the injury list simultaneously meant Brabin got busy in the transfer window, signing strikers Stuart Fleetwood (Hereford) and Collin Samuel (free agent), plus Southport's pocket-sized midfield trickster John-Paul Kissock. He shipped out Barnes-Homer, Poku and Walker on loan, and rejected Stevenage and Forest Green bids for Keane and Willmott respectively. The revolving doors at Kenilworth Road were spinning at speed, and it was tough keeping track 0f it all.

September 2011: Pain of the Self-Inflicted Sort

Plucking draws from the jaws of victory was becoming a bad habit at Luton. The contest at Stockport County, live on satellite television, featured a superb 5th-minute piledriver from Lawless, but it was a goal Luton could not add to, no matter how they tried. Then, in stoppage time, McConville's shot deflected past Tyler off Asafu-Adjaye, and debutant sub Fleetwood hit a post with the last kick of the game. It all meant two more points had slipped away.

Jamie Hand arrived on loan from Hayes and Yeading to debut in a comfortable 2-0 win over Darlington, with Crow opening the scoring in the first half from Fleetwood's cross. The visitors' Lee was red carded before Fleetwood bagged the second after a corner. The rearranged AFC Telford trip three days later saw Luton end with ten men after Asafu-Adjaye picked up two cautions, but Morgan-Smith had by then converted a Willmott cross and rifled a second from 18 yards. The 2-0 win pushed us up to third.

We had to make do again with ten men on the following Saturday at home to Lincoln, skipper Beckwith given marching orders halfway through the goalless first period. A superb second-half display was capped by great work on the left by Kissock, allowing Fleetwood to flick a jubilant 84th-minute winner, leaving the ground rocking and preserving the unbeaten record. Kissock was a former Everton prodigy, whose extravagant skills were establishing him as a real favourite as we soared up to second. The flicks, the step-overs and the 'Cruyff turns' seemed to be a standard part of his game, and although it was tempting to think he over-egged things sometimes, he did raise a smile and a cheer virtually every time he got the ball. Some reckoned he was a showboater, but football is supposed to be entertaining isn't it?

With Beckwith banned and other defenders injured, Janos Kovács returned to the club for a second loan spell, going straight into the side at

Bath. We dominated possession and Morgan-Smith netted a rebound when Fleetwood's shot was saved, but we failed to press home our advantage and Phillips levelled. Bath played 50 minutes with ten men and towards the end dropped down to nine, Stonehouse adding to Clough's red card, but they hung on to 1-1. This definitely felt like points dropped, despite the fact we went top of the table thanks to results elsewhere going in our favour. It was the classic Luton paradox: we went top for the first time in more than a year, yet players, fans and management all headed home up the M4 feeling thoroughly dissatisfied.

If Bath was a downer, the outcome at York just four days later was nothing short of calamitous. An atrocious first half saw a reshuffled and injury-hit Luton looking all at sea, and we conceded three times – Chambers (two) and former Hatter Walker doing the damage. The home side were sharper and hungrier, and although Town improved after the break, the damage was done. The 3-0 loss represented our heaviest defeat in the last 124 league and Conference games. Kissock and Lawless were missing for the second half. The former ran out of steam having been unwell before the game, while the latter ludicrously broke a bone in his hand during the interval, punching a wall in anger at how things were going against his former club. Although such passion was admirable, self-inflicted problems were the last thing the team needed at that point. Lawless put himself out of action for weeks and was disciplined by the club as a result.

Brabin called the whole Bootham Crescent farrago an absolute disaster, and chairman Nick Owen admitted to being 'shrouded in bewildered gloom'. He wasn't the only one. The defeat dropped us out of the play-off zone on goal difference, but the chance to get back on track came three days later with a visit from Cambridge United. Luton were on top in the first period, but after McAuley headed the Us in front on the hour mark, things went downhill and we failed to find the ideas and energy to claw things back. The crowd made its feelings known at the end and no wonder, for we were down to ninth place in the table, surprise packets Gateshead and Braintree now leading the way.

October 2011: Chelsea Fan Successfully Converted

The anxiety and frustration of the last three games leaked into the opening 10 minutes of October's action. After just 74 seconds of Barrow's visit, teenager Mackreth chipped a smart goal right in front of a disbelieving Kenilworth stand. Then Willmott looked to have spurned the chance of a quick equaliser when his penalty was pushed against a post by Hurst. Thankfully, he reacted quickly to knock in the rebound. It proved a turning point, and from here it became one-way traffic towards the Barrow goal. We had to wait until the second half for goals by Willmott, Watkins, Dance and Morgan-Smith to give proceedings a realistic 5-1 scoreline.

A week later, with the injury list now diminishing, good approach play by Morgan-Smith set up two goals for Willmott at Kidderminster, and Luton survived a late fightback to come away 2-1 winners. It was no coincidence that central defenders Blackett and Pilkington were making their first appearances of the season. We even had the luxury of fit senior players watching from the stands.

A midweek trip to Ebbsfleet, toilers at the foot of the Conference coalface, saw another two-goal lead forged, Morgan-Smith's majestic shot added to by Dance. But, as per Saturday, the closing minutes proved stressful, the home side launching a desperate bid to get on terms, encouraged by a 76th minute goal. More than 700 Luton fans watched in horror as our resistance crumbled and West bagged an equaliser right at the death. Carden was making a rare appearance in place of suspended Keane, and it was he who copped the brunt of the fans' anger at this night's outcome. Carden had been barracked by many from day one, apparently his critics believing he was only recruited through being an old pal of the manager. Tonight's abuse was unusually intense and prompted a reaction from the Luton boardroom. Gary Sweet revealed the manager of a League club witnessed the barracking and told him, 'You're going nowhere with that lot dragging you down. I've never seen that before. How can you play every week in front of that aggression?'

Acknowledging that the majority of Luton fans would have found the barracking 'embarrassing', Sweet made the valid point that it was picked up by the Ebbsfleet players, who revelled in the opportunity to use it to their advantage. He said,

> [Carden] never has been and will never be our enemy. He was not responsible for our last administration or the deduction of 40 points; was certainly not responsible for the reason we haven't got promoted in the last two seasons, and not accountable for [this] loss of two points.

Recent events had made it seem like one step forward and two steps back for Luton's promotion cause. The roller-coaster ride duly continued four days later when well-placed Gateshead were torn apart 5-1 at Kenilworth Road. It put the home fans in fine voice, none more tuneful than singer and broadcaster Cerys Matthews, who reported that this game's excitement persuaded her son to switch from being a Chelsea fan to a Luton fan. She took him into Luton's club shop and that also helped her mission to convert him, she revealed. Good work, Cerys.

It was plain sailing after O'Connor had bagged his first goal for the club; Howells netted a well-taken brace and Hand unexpectedly popped up with two cracking efforts. At the end of a very satisfactory afternoon's work, Brabin was seen deep in conversation with Gateshead marksman Jon Shaw in the centre circle: perhaps he was to be our next signing?

With sixteen games gone we were up to third, a point behind Fleetwood and five behind Wrexham, who came to Kenilworth Road three days later. A bumper gate of 7,270 turned out to see the battle of the high-fliers, but the visitors were not here to entertain, and their rugged, cautious approach proved hard to counter. In a game of few chances, a counter-attack was poorly dealt with by Luton's rearguard and the West African Pogba nipped in to slide home a winning goal. It was a lesson for Luton in how to 'win ugly'. Brabin evidently took it on board and, to our surprise, Luton managed something similar in the following game, away at Grimsby.

To provide muscle in attack alongside the nippy Fleetwood and O'Connor, big Tommy Wright had joined on a short-term deal. He demonstrated his prowess in front of a live television audience at Blundell Park, sinking his former Mariners teammates in the process. A deft, flicked cross by Fleetwood was powered home by the tattooed Wright for the only goal of the game on 73 minutes. Fewer than 200 Luton fans saw the win in person, but the loyalists who made it to Humberside enjoyed their fish and chips in the very mild, un-Grimsby-like weather.

The points ensured Luton kept pace with the chasing pack immediately behind Wrexham and Fleetwood, who were showing signs of breaking away from the rest. It was unrelenting high-pressure stuff, but now we had an FA Cup fourth qualifying round tie against Hendon to allow a timely rest for some senior men. Fringe players were called up to sample 'the magic of the Cup', and a comfy 5-1 win featured Charlie Henry making a belated debut after a year of injury. It was not all good news, however, for in heading the second goal Dance spoiled his male-model looks by fracturing a cheekbone and eye socket. O'Connor (2), Wright and Fleetwood snapped up the others and we waltzed through to a home tie with Northampton in the first round proper.

November 2011: All Alone in the Centre Circle

Gary Brabin had now served more than six months in charge, and although his evolving squad certainly looked strong enough to be 'in the mix' when the season drew to a close, there were major reservations among fans over whether we'd ever be in with a shout of the title itself. Having been unable to outmanoeuvre current leaders Wrexham recently, the second big test was now upon us, a visit from second-placed Fleetwood.

The visitors spent heavily in the summer (Vardy, Brodie, et al.) and had genuine belief the Football League was within reach, even though this was only their second season at this level. Four promotions in seven years showed what heavy investment could bring. The match was a torrid, high tempo affair, bad tempered throughout and the visitors posed Luton plenty of problems. After 11 minutes, everybody hesitated expecting a free-kick, but Vardy played to the whistle and cut in from the left flank to chip a neat opening goal. A half of utter frustration ended with shenanigans in the tunnel, Fleetwood players, management and the officials all getting it in the neck from unhappy home fans. Quite what went on under the tunnel's canvas roof remained a mystery, but it nearly broke free of its moorings.

After the break, a Milligan penalty took the game further from our grasp. Morgan-Smith struck the bar with a fine shot, but our only reward was a Kovács header in the dying seconds – too little, too late. The defeat dropped us to seventh and the natives were more than just restless. Brabin left no stone unturned to try and improve things, sending Henry, Lacey, Antwi and Tavernier out on loan, releasing Samuel and long-term injury victim Murray – all of which allowed us to bring in young Stoke striker Ryan Brunt on a work experience deal, Darlington full-back Greg Taylor on loan and to extend the arrangement with Hand.

The FA Cup provided a welcome distraction with Northampton providing 'local derby' opposition from the League. The Cobblers attempted to play expansive football, unlike the vast majority of our Conference visitors. An intriguing contest was settled by the only goal, a dramatic late effort by sub Watkins, who fired home first time from the edge of the area. First-half injuries to key men Morgan-Smith and Keane was bad news, but the real turmoil was in our visitors' camp – they had now won just seven games from thirty-four since Gary Johnson took charge, so it wasn't hugely surprising to hear his departure announced less than forty-eight hours after this defeat.

A trip to the Abbey Stadium followed, with 1,754 travelling fans seeing Luton impress in the first half, encouraged by an early goal from Fleetwood. The lead was held for at least an hour, but an important win was yanked from our grip when Hughes netted a far-post equaliser. Yet more points dropped from a winning position. Later that evening, BBC's *Match of the Day* analysed an incident involving Blackburn Rovers, in which they got away with something that Luton were pulled up for at Cambridge.

Rovers' forward Morten Gamst Pedersen was spotted by the cameras taking a short corner with himself to set up a Blackburn goal. A few hours earlier, the much smaller audience at the Abbey Stadium had witnessed our very own Stuart Fleetwood kick off after Cambridge's equaliser by touching the ball to himself. Now, Pedersen's action was surely a case of deliberate cheating (as the television pundits pointed out), whereas Fleetwood's manoeuvre had merely been the desperate action of a man who found himself all alone at the centre spot. Young sub Brunt had been there a moment earlier, but mysteriously sprinted off to the left flank, leaving Fleets to get on with the job alone. Unlike the ref at Blackburn, our official at Cambridge had his wits about him and pulled Luton up. It was a bizarre moment and one that many people missed, judging by the puzzled looks when Cambridge were given an indirect free-kick.

Conceding that 77th-minute equaliser was a massive blow to the bumper turnout of travelling Luton fans, for the excellent first-half display had seen us knock the ball about nicely, just like Luton sides of the past. If only O'Connor (dressing room nickname 'Azzer') had not stumbled when clean through with the chance to make it 0-2. His hard running was impressive, however, and he had genuine pace. We looked a very decent team for an hour, well balanced and dangerous going forward, but were less potent after the interval. Once again, fans were left depressed by the lack of a big final push in the last 15 minutes, something that, in years gone by, always seemed to be a feature of Luton games. Perhaps the absence of Keane meant we had just run out of energy?

Looking at the BSP table that Saturday night was a painful experience. We were now nine points behind Wrexham and Fleetwood, two teams who failed to impress me, but who did seem to know how to close out a game when leading. A week later, in difficult conditions at Newport, a fighting Luton display in a swirling wind ended with Dance setting up Crow for a 93rd-minute last-gasp winner, jubilantly received by the hardy 271 who made the long journey. Skipper Pilkington talked optimistically of this hard-earned win being a turning point – 'the one to get our season going' – and we desperately hoped he was right when lowly AFC Telford came to Luton three days later.

We applied early pressure, the visitors weathering the storm until shortly before half-time, when Willmott powered home a loose ball. A superb, curling 25-yard free-kick from Newton then levelled matters and Andy Sinton's men hung on for a draw, celebrating with gusto at the end. It was now three home games without a win for the Hatters and the lack of sharpness in front of goal was all too familiar.

December 2011: M'learned Friend Hits the Deck

The visit of League Two side Cheltenham in the second round of the FA Cup meant season ticket holders like myself could pay on the gate and try a different seat for a change. I opted for one high in the Main Stand, where the leg room is like Easy Jet's planes but the view includes a panorama of the Chiltern Hills. Sadly, the view from this angle also accentuated the fact Gleeson was moving at a pace that suggested he was not quite match fit (I normally sit at pitch level where everybody looks fast and nippy, even the big fellas). I also had a clear view of Kissock trying to worm his way through, only to be knocked over by Cheltenham's Duffy, who got a red card and then appeared to claim he'd been the victim of mistaken identity. Luckily, the boys from ITV Sport zoomed in later on and proved justice had been done. We matched Cheltenham for most of the game, but they were sharper in front of goal. With Dance not selected, the winger's infamous lucky FA Cup jacket was unable to weave its usual magic. Brabin must have forgotten about this when he named his team. The jacket featured prominently on social media before the game, but its owner stayed unused on the subs bench. An entertaining tie ended in a 2-4 defeat, but we enjoyed two O'Connor goals and much praise from the visiting manager and ITV commentators. Such was the desperation to sort out our league future that these Cup defeats didn't really feel too depressing; the only really annoying thing about the whole weekend proved to be the news that Cheltenham's reward for beating us was a third-round tie with Spurs.

So, instead of going toe-to-toe with Tottenham, our next cup action was far more prosaic – Swindon Supermarine at home in the FA Trophy. A goal in each half by Fleetwood and Wright saw us through, but eight team changes from the previous line-up and just 1,298 in the ground told the real story. Incidentally, ITV's Cup coverage this week flagged up the story that rivals Wrexham were now fully under the control of their own supporters trust. This was great news for the game in general, a victory for true fans over dodgy owners. We were experts on this topic at Luton. However, any goodwill towards the men from North Wales quickly disappeared when Brentford boss Uwe Rosler revealed in a post-match interview that Wrexham's players liked to go in for screaming and ranting in the tunnel, an intimidating tactic that was introduced by that uncouth Wimbledon mob of the 1980s. How classy.

Next up, Luton produced a patchy Conference display at Lincoln, increasing the sense of frustration in the camp. Crow gave us a lead that was pegged back by a physical home side that upped their game considerably after the interval. Having lost Pilkington early, his substitute Hand was red carded later on, adding to the departure of Lawless for two cautions. It meant the final stages of a game that was there for the winning saw us desperately protecting a point with only nine men.

The Bedfordshire natives were restless again – and no wonder. Christmas was coming, we were almost halfway through the campaign and were struggling to break into the top five, not to mention a long way adrift of the leaders. This was not promotion form and, looking back, it's hard to see where any real progress was made in the two and a quarter years after Mick Harford was deemed unfit for the task of taking us forward.

Current manager Brabin is many things, but a natural-born cyclist he is surely not. So rumours that he'd suffered 'an accident on his bike' and would miss an appearance before Selby Magistrates Court as a result, did have a ring of truth about them. It was easy to imagine Brabs getting into difficulty when negotiating the busy Dunstable Road and A505 relief road on two wheels as he pedalled to work. It is easy to imagine him taking a tumble in all that busy pre-Christmas traffic. However, we were soon officially informed it was all nonsense, and the manager's barrister was the man who had hit the tarmac. M'learned friend got his silks caught in his pedals perhaps? The LTFC hierarchy sounded a little annoyed that such stories were doing the rounds, but it was probably all due to a 'silly season' created by an idle eleven-day gap between league games. Instead of proper football over this period, we got the FA Trophy, which was a non-event as far as most Luton fans were concerned. The prospect of a second-round tie at Hinckley wouldn't change that situation either.

Tamworth away on the Saturday before Christmas was hardly a mouth-watering prospect either, yet an impressive total of 622 made the journey. They were rewarded with an attacking display featuring sixteen shots on goal and the sight of a team clearly determined not to fritter away another lead. A controversial early red card for home defender Green for his tackle on Gleeson helped the cause, Crow hooking us ahead from a corner despite nearly having the shirt ripped off his back in the process. Early in the second half, fine shots by Crow and Dance made the net billow right in front of the away fans, and it was party time as we enjoyed a 3-0 comfort zone. Francis also saw red for fouling Keane, but Crow missed the resultant penalty and the chance of a hat-trick. When the home side nicked a consolation goal, all of a sudden it was 1-3 instead of the more realistic 0-4. Nevertheless, the points were well deserved and we enjoyed the rare sight of a Luton team firing on all cylinders across 90 minutes instead of just in patches.

The chance to build on this and boost confidence further came on Boxing Day, when crisis club Kettering were yuletide visitors. One thing we could be sure about was that the Poppies would definitely not 'park the bus', as Jose Mourinho likes to call it. Why? Because they hadn't got one. Not only that, they couldn't afford to hire one either. The Poppies players were told to make their own way to Luton for the game, because the club was so hard up it couldn't afford to provide transport. This conjured up all sorts of amusing images of young men with kit bags dashing up and down the cramped streets of Bury Park, desperately trying to find the players' entrance at Kenilworth Road. It is not an easy one to locate.

Boxing Day has produced some colourful Luton Town occasions down the years. This time it was notable for giving us the most one-sided league fixture ever seen at Kenilworth Road. It wasn't a classic by any means, but the gulf in class between the sides was gigantic. Never mind the quality, feel the width. There were five goals, a series of near-things, a missed penalty, even the odd air shot, in 90 minutes of one-way traffic, enjoyed to the full by a jovial and well-stuffed crowd of more than 7,000. O'Connor was the latest guilty party from the spot, smashing his attempt against the bar. Brabin claimed they did practice penalties in training, but the astonishing list of recent misses proved how fragile our confidence could be in pressure situations. Short on cash, short on substitutes and banned from signing new faces, beleagured Kettering were so outclassed it was almost embarrassing.

Their ageing skipper, the former Luton legend Sol Davis, was a pale shadow of his old self, but did his best to look like a seasoned old pro whose know-how made up for a lack of fitness. He barely broke into a run all game, and his only real contribution was to make one good clearance off the line. What a pity Mr Dance wasn't playing, or anybody else who could have given him a roasting down the flank. Sol ambled around and was repeatedly applauded by home fans on the rare occasion he got possession – what a generous lot we were. Funnily enough, the Poppies' best player on the day was another ex-Hatter, Stephen O'Leary, who at least looked like he was trying, but didn't get a fraction of the recognition afforded Sol. Five classy goals and some comedic misses kept us well entertained. Kettering never stood a chance and were even short on the coaching front, manager Mark Stimson looking a bit like Nobby No-Mates in the dugout. Seeing a club on the verge of going bust was no laughing matter, but Kettering chairman Imraan Ladak had raised a chuckle by claiming admission prices for the return game had not been raised by an astronomic 60 per cent simply because a high turnout of Luton fans was expected. Would he really have increased prices from £12 to £19 if it had been Alfreton or Braintree showing up on New Year's Day and not Luton Town? I doubt it. The Poppies' problems intensified recently when the club was unable to pay the players in full, leading to some not turning up for training. Since then they've gone ten games without a win and slipped to twenty-second in the table. Having already lost their stadium, a transfer embargo means they have had to field non-contract and youth team players. The future looks grim.

We do love Boxing Day at Luton. In the last four decades or so, I can only recall one really bad one – the occasion when Colchester beat us 4-1 in a strange encounter in which we had all the possession but were toothless in attack. Best Boxing Days were a couple of victories over Watford and the one where we nicked a 1-0 at league leaders Ipswich in 1974 – my first Luton away match. Bobby Robson's men dominated but simply couldn't score. With 90-plus minutes on the clock, Luton broke forward and won a rare corner. Aston's kick swirled over, diminutive home 'keeper Sivell (imagine Kissock with gloves) flapped desperately, and teenage debutant R. Futcher rose to power in the winner with his head. It is incredible to think the likes of veteran Sol Davis weren't even born back then!

January 2012: Christmas Gifts That Kept on Giving

As it was holiday time, the fixture gurus kindly paired us with the same local opposition twice in five days, so on New Year's Day we travelled to Kettering's temporary home Nene Park. Perhaps it should be renamed Groundhog Day, for most of the stats from the first meeting were repeated: 5-0 to Luton by the end, having been 2-0 up at half-time, and five different scorers (Howells, Watkins, Kovács, Taylor, Fleetwood). Sixty per cent possession and twenty-three shots on goal for Luton was also remarkably similar to the Boxing Day stats. Hapless Kettering struggled to even fill their subs bench, so could ill afford to go down to ten men when Ifil earned a red card for an assault on Taylor. A bumper turnout of more than 2,000 Luton fans paid through the nose to get into Nene Park to enjoy the fun, making up almost two thirds of the entire attendance. We were up to third in the table – albeit a massive eleven points behind leaders Wrexham – but the transfer window had opened and optimism was in the air again. In-form loanees Kovács and Taylor were converted into permanent transfers, while Barnes-Homer and Antwi quietly left the club.

With Justin Edinburgh in charge, we had a good idea of what to expect when Newport visited Kenilworth Road, and he didn't let us down. They succeeded in shutting down our creative outlets and quietened the crowd for a good half hour before a sending-off changed the game. Former Hatter Charles caught Gleeson with a late tackle and departed, the breakthrough goal coming just minutes later when O'Connor deftly headed in Howells' cross. County posed no real threat themselves, but were tough to break down. All was well once a good move ended with Crow netting at the far post for 2-0, injuring himself in the process.

Three days later, we ground out a fifth successive league win against Stockport, who were scrambling hard to get free of the drop zone now that Jim Gannon had replaced manager Dietmar Hamann. Gannon had introduced ten new faces in eight weeks, and although County had only won four times all season, they hadn't come to Luton to roll over. There was a subdued atmosphere, not helped by losing the toss and kicking towards a near-empty Oak Road in the second half. Whether or not he'd been lurking in the corridor on a deliberate spying mission remains unclear, but our coach Carden said he actually heard instructions being issued in the away dressing room to 'make sure the crowd gets on Luton's back'. After a dull first half, tactical changes by Brabin eventually paid off. The lively Watkins was tripped and sub O'Connor coolly registered our first spot-kick success for some time.

FA Trophy second-round business with Hinckley United passed almost unnoticed in mid-January, a 0-0 in the Midlands followed by a routine 3-0 replay win, the two ties attracting less than 1,800 between them. Some of the younger squad players were given a go in the spotlight. And on the subject of youth, it was announced that Chelsea had passed on some of their cash in exchange for three of our academy kids, the Dasilva brothers (Rio, Cole and Jay). If they made it through the Stamford Bridge system into the first team, it was reported Luton would benefit to the tune of over £1 million. The deal was regarded at Kenilworth Road as a positive development, mainly because in this cut-throat world there was a danger we might have lost them for nothing. The Dasilva boys trundled off a LTFC conveyor belt that was also trodden by top-division stars such as Jack Wilshere, Emerson Boyce, Matthew Taylor, Matthew Upson, Kevin Foley, Curtis Davies and Leon Barnett.

As far as incoming players were concerned, Luton seemed to be getting through strikers like Rod Stewart used to get through blondes. Brabin's latest punt was to release Wright after just three months and replace him with Scotsman Craig McAllister, borrowed from Newport. In this age of multiple loan deals, McAllister was yet another thirty-something qualifying for the label 'journeyman'. His record in front of goal was not prolific (even Everton goalkeeper Howard had scored more this season), but according to Luton fan and former player Andy Burgess, McAllister was useful with his back to goal, and good at bringing others into the game. If he struck up a partnership with Fleetwood, the headline writers would no doubt refer to 'Fleetwood Mac' hitting the right notes.

Luton's winning run (not counting cup ties) ended with a lively 3-3 draw at Southport, a howling gale playing a key role in proceedings. In a game he'd want to forget, Pilkington ended up diving the wrong way as the wind helped Gray's strike from distance put us behind. Mukendi doubled the lead before a close-range Crow header gave hope. After the break, well-taken efforts by Watkins and O'Connor completed a superb comeback, but the celebrations were cut short when unlucky Pilkington saw a shot go in off his heel after flying at him off a post. The former Manchester United 'keeper had been Brabin's first choice since November, but surely today's calamities would see a return for the evergreen Tyler?

Further frustration followed four days later when the goals dried up at home to Mansfield – our first goalless game of the season, but the eleventh draw in thirty league games. It is remarkable how often we failed to produce the goods whenever live television cameras come along. Injury-prone marksman Morgan-Smith made his first league start since the autumn but departed in pain before the hour mark. Debutant McAllister couldn't find a way through either, and we were left offering thanks to centre-back Pilkington for two goalline clearances, without which it would have been a very sorry evening indeed. The skipper was hero of the hour again at the end of the same week, popping home the winning goal against relegation battlers Alfreton with a first-half penalty. This fifth 1-0 win of the season maintained the pace of our challenge, but it was an unmemorable contest, the only real goalmouth excitement coming in the dying seconds.

We now entered the final third of the season, and despite being some way behind Fleetwood and Wrexham, looked well established in the play-off zone. Nevertheless, there was still edginess and tension about much of our play. In readiness for the run-in, Brabin sealed a deal on deadline day to bring York's Andre Boucaud to Kenilworth Road, coughing up £25,000 for a man he felt could bring a stylish new dimension to our midfield.

February 2012: Why Mascots Don't Run Marathons

Snow and frozen conditions took their toll, and several games fell by the wayside. The squad were forced to head for Dunstable to use 3G pitches for training. This unscheduled mid-season break saw us go three weeks without a league fixture, meaning that by the time of Tamworth's visit, our unbeaten run stood at twelve games and fifteen weeks.

The break left fans anxious and irritable from missing their weekly football fix, but on the other hand provided the opportunity to use weekends in other ways. One Hatters season ticket holder, Chris Beard, channeled his energies into a weird and wonderful event called the Enigma Quadzilla in Milton Keynes. It involved running four marathons in four days. In recent years, supporting Luton has certainly needed patience, an iron will and bags of stamina. The terraces at Luton must be a good breeding ground for marathon runners.

Although this writer has never attempted anything quite as insane as the Quadzilla weekend, I do recall the time I planned to run the London Marathon dressed as 'Kenilworth the Cat'. The cat was the official club mascot at Luton back then, in the days before being replaced by Happy Harry with his big head and funny feet. In conjunction with Luton's commercial manager Mike Beevor (an ex-international runner) it was arranged I would run the 26.2-mile race in the official furry Kenilworth costume. I collected it on a match day, an hour or two after it had been used, and took it away in order to get familiar with the act of running along clothed in something totally unfit for purpose. Having got the huge, smelly garment home, and been banned by the wife from bringing it indoors, it soon dawned what a completely mental idea this was.

The costume was heavy, uncomfortable and extremely hot, and exactly the sort of thing a well-honed athlete like myself should not be running inside. I discreetly took the costume out of town to a quiet country lane, ready to do my impersonation of the local village idiot. I hoped my practice session wouldn't be seen by too many passers-by, especially if they supported a club other than Luton. Luckily, there was nobody around to witness this giant cat running down the road on its hind legs. Doing this alone on a quiet Wednesday for a few minutes was one thing, doing it for four hours in crowded Central London on marathon day would be quite another. I'd barely trotted 400 yards before accepting it was mission impossible. The heat generated inside was incredible.

These were the early days of football mascot costumes, and I suspect modern ones are far better in terms of comfort, ventilation and portability. To cut a long story short, Kenilworth the Cat was returned to Kenilworth Road, and I ran the marathon in Luton playing kit instead. Not only was it more comfortable, the reaction it drew from the crowds (some positive, some negative) certainly kept my mind off the pain of running a marathon.

But I digress. Back to the gruelling winter of 2011/12, and the weather relented enough to allow Luton to make progress in the FA Trophy. Kidderminster were beaten 2-1 at Aggborough – an impressive display on a bitter night, only marred by yet another missed penalty (the seventh this season). This time, Fleetwood was the offender. When we finally got back to the more important Conference action, Brabin went for skill rather than muscle against Tamworth, picking Kissock and debutant Boucaud to start, even though the rain was thrashing down grimly on our humble home in the Chiltern foothills. It was an interesting team selection, because this clearly wouldn't be a day for lightweights. Hyperactive Fleetwood poached a goal to put us ahead, prior to a lengthy power cut, which thankfully didn't force abandonment. Kovács headed the important second goal and later tried to claim another, but the eagle-eyed spotted that it went in off Francis' shins for an own goal. This comfortable 3-0 win against mediocre opposition kept things ticking over, but elsewhere Fleetwood and Wrexham both won again, meaning we were still failing to make inroads into their lead.

Brabin tried to paint an optimistic picture of our title chances, saying he was happy for the time being that Fleetwood and Wrexham were keeping each other fully occupied, as it meant Luton could quietly gather points while waiting for them to slip up. It didn't cut much ice with most Luton fans, who were resigned to another play-off battle as long as we held our nerve and didn't collapse in the final fourteen games or so. It became even more widely accepted that first place was out of reach when we made the long trip to Barrow, a game rescheduled for a Tuesday night, and went down by the only goal of an awful game. Inevitably, the wind was fierce, the rain tumbled down, the dodgy pitch was cut up badly, the opposition were over-physical and the referee inept. These were the type of games we had to get used to, and found so difficult to deal with.

Occasionally, tempers frayed and Luton frustration hit new heights when Barrow's Harvey buried the winning goal past Tyler with less than 20 minutes left. The attendance was announced as a miserable 925, some seventy of them visiting fans, although those who were present swore there were well over 100 away fans. Free scarves were given out to the Luton loyalists by our management, a nice gesture in recognition that nights like this one were about as bad as it got. It was our first defeat in thirteen league games, but that was hardly any consolation.

Following Barrow's bully-boy tactics, the FA Trophy quarter-final tie at Kenilworth Road with Gateshead was at least refreshing in that both sides tried to play proper football. Early on, Kissock volleyed his first goal for the club past a goalkeeper rooted to the spot, and on the hour mark Keane swung in a free-kick towards the far post and saw it end up in the net to clinch victory. Wembley crept a little closer, although we were given the toughest possible semi-final draw, paired with play-off rivals York.

March 2012: Making Hot Work of Bath Time

So to the season's pivotal month, the one where a team with genuine ambition either accelerates into the home straight, consolidates, or merely falls away. Not much margin for error in March. The fun got underway when Bath City were our visitors, bottom of the table by some distance. Judging by the jokes about them being a shower, and on their way down the plughole, Bath would surely be prime cannon fodder, and this game would surely be a great opportunity for McAllister to break his scoring duck.

Everybody feels bad for a striker such as McAllister on a goalless run, who simply couldn't score whenever he tried. Our man was in good company though, and I find myself pondering which barren spell would end first – that of Fernando Torres or Craig McAllister. Perhaps Luton fan Graham Sharpe, a senior executive at William Hill bookmakers, would have to be consulted on this one. Torres and McAllister were both mired in dreadful runs of more than twenty games each since they last hit the onion bag. The bookies had Torres down at 7/4 to net at West Brom this weekend, while McAllister was 7/2 to bag the first in our match with Bath.

I rarely bet on Luton Town matters these days, not with real money anyway, for as we all know they are not easy to call. It would probably be easier to predict the attendance against Bath than it would the scoreline and scorers. I think the last time I placed hard-earned wonga on the outcome of a Hatters game was way back in 1989, when I put a hefty sum on us beating Nottingham Forest in the League Cup final at Wembley. The odds were, I felt, very generous for what was essentially a two-horse race. I shan't name the sum, but I have to admit not holding back when the wallet came out in William Hill's that week. Subsequently, for about an hour of that game, I had pound signs flashing in front of my eyes. Then the late, great Les Sealey did his kamikaze challenge on Nigel Clough and we were done for. Game over, penury beckoned.

Luton made hard work of Bath, and it took goals at either end of the game by Kovács and Watkins to ensure three points. It was not exactly a happy afternoon, the team was booed off at half time and Brabin talking afterwards about players not adhering to his game plan and over-elaborating on the ball. The fans expected better than this and were continuing to show it. There was little real optimism four days later when we attempted to close the widening gap on that night's opponents, Wrexham. And our fourth appearance on live television that season, under the Racecourse floodlights, duly proved a miserable affair. It was a classic case of a team trying to play football being outmuscled by a side making the most of limited but well-organised assets. The game was over before half-time, when the Welshmen went two-up with Luton having rarely threatened. The final straw was Kissock's red card after he rashly rose to the bait of Wrexham's over-physical midfield.

There was a visible improvement the following Saturday as the club bid for its seventh Wembley appearance, this time by way of the FA Trophy and a first-leg semi-final tie at York. Strange things tend to happen when these clubs meet, so Luton were well advised to keep Lawless away from any brick walls and Brabin away from any stewards. The inevitable red card came when Howells handled inside the area on 13 minutes, and York netted the penalty. Our ten men held out and were reduced to nine when Keane committed two bookable tackles within 2 minutes and was also shown red. The remaining heroes rolled their sleeves up and somehow kept it at 1-0, a five-star performance from Tyler in particular. It meant massive plaudits for a 1-0 defeat, hot on the heels of jeers for beating Bath 2-0. It sure is a strange old world following Luton.

What followed saw us grateful to grasp a single point at crisis-club Darlington. We lost Kovács to another red card, fell a goal behind but levelled in the last minute through Fleetwood. Then, dramatically, a penalty was awarded to the home side in mysterious circumstances in the dying seconds. Tyler came to the rescue and saved it, meaning justice was surely served and we could trek home reasonably pleased. Mind you, there was nothing to celebrate about the league table – we were still third but now twenty points adrift of second-placed Wrexham, and facing a tight battle with three other clubs for the remaining three play-off places.

The Trophy semi-final second leg with bogey side York saw a much improved first-half display, culminating in Willmott levelling the aggregate scores just before the break. It was nip and tuck from then on until the 90th minute, when the need for extra time vanished as Blair headed in at the far post to take the Minstermen to Wembley. Amazingly, this was the first goal conceded in eleven home games, but a more annoying statistic was that we'd now only beaten York once in ten contests since dropping out of the League.

Brabin has broad shoulders, which was just as well, for many minds were by now made up – the very vocal campaign to have him removed was gathering momentum. The final straw for many fans came at Forest Green three days later when a dreadful display ended in a 3-0 mauling by a side barely halfway in the table, and in front of a meagre crowd of 975. The hangover from the York disappointment added to a general atmosphere of dissatisfaction and produced a lacklustre performance that left poor Brabin ashamed and apologetic. Skipper Pilkington, too, reckoned 'it was not merely a bad day at the office, but far worse than that'.

The writing was on the wall for the beleaguered manager as MD Gary Sweet addressed the fan base a few days later with commendable frankness: 'Ladies and gentlemen, what we have delivered recently has not been acceptable.' His lengthy statement went on to suggest that Brabin – popular and well-liked as a man, but failing to deliver as a manager – was on some sort of final warning and only a dramatic improvement and run of victories could now save him. However, action was being taken to rectify things and the highly rated striker Andre Gray arrived at the club for £30,000 from Hinckley, quickly followed by former midfielder Lil Fuccillo, named as the club's new technical director. Fuccillo's role was said to be advisory and he was definitely not a new manager-in-waiting, we were assured.

The next day, Grimsby, one of a handful jostling to keep us out of the top five places, visited the red-hot cauldron of discontent that was Kenilworth Road. Debutant Gray volleyed us ahead and showed great potential, which improved the general mood until an 87th-minute equaliser was drilled in by Grimsby's Hughes-Mason. It was now six games without a win and we slipped out of the play-off zone. Brabin was surely entering the last chance saloon when his nemesis York (again) arrived at Kenilworth Road to round off a month of traumatic action.

These two teams had identical records, disliked each other with a passion, and if ever there was a true six-pointer, this was it. The game proved another roller-coaster ride for Hatters fans. After just 5 minutes, Gray's blistering speed took him past surprised defenders to crash home a fine goal from a narrow angle. A lively contest ensued, both sides going close, the match coming to a dramatic climax in the final 10 minutes. York won a hotly disputed free kick on the byeline, which was fed to unmarked McLaughlin to equalise from 18 yards. For the umpteenth time in recent history, we were beaten in the late stages when a save by Tyler rebounded for Meredith to tuck in a heart-breaking 85th-minute winner. It was lively fare for the television cameras, and they came up with a stunning moment of poignancy at the end of two hours of coverage: a camera positioned inside the tunnel lingered on the lonely, thoughtful figure of Brabin as he looked out on a deserted stadium. A picture tells a thousand words. One wonders whether this shot was staged with Brabin's permission, or was it genuinely a man being secretly filmed as he said a private farewell to his place of work?

The winless run of seven games had dropped Luton out of the top five and there were only seven games left. The one automatic promotion place was long gone, and now a play-off berth looked unlikely. These bare facts, along with the recent Forest Green humiliation, did indeed prove to be the end of the line. Gary Brabin's departure was duly announced the following day.

April 2012: Some Very Uncomfortable Viewing

Assistant Alan Neilson was in caretaker charge for the next match at Braintree, even though bookies' favourite Paul Buckle was unveiled as manager the day before the game in Essex. Buckle, brought up a few miles outside Luton, appeared to have similar qualifications as his predecessor. He had a modest career as a midfielder with various lower division clubs, and as a manager led Torquay to promotion from the Conference in 2009, but then followed a short and unhappy spell in charge of Bristol Rovers. He was young and keen, but watching his new club from the rickety little stand at Braintree must have made uncomfortable viewing. He sat making copious notes. They would have made interesting reading.

Those who suggested the game at Forest Green had been a new low point in Luton Town history suddenly had a new candidate for that accolade. Braintree's humble surroundings just off the A120 in mid-Essex, their status as part-timers, the uneven pitch and lack of atmosphere were all key ingredients. Mix these with the way Luton caved in meekly to a 1-3 reverse and you had new and embarrassing depths being plumbed. The less said about this debacle the better, but at least Buckle had been given an early chance to see for himself how bad things had got. Three fundamentals were plainly missing: confidence, motivation and organisation.

Buckle took full control and launched the new era at the club forty-eight hours later against Hayes and Yeading at home. He'd had very little time to work with his new charges, but fans were demanding an instant improvement. Surely things could only get better from here? The darkest hour comes before the dawn and all that? In more than six weeks we'd only collected a meagre five league points, meaning we now needed other clubs to slip up as well as chalk up wins ourselves. If not, the unthinkable would become reality – we would be condemned to a fourth year in non-League hell, this time without even the excitement of play-offs.

Easter Monday brought blessed relief as blue-shirted Hayes were seen off 4-2, two cracking goals by Fleetwood in the first period banishing lingering tension. Gray's fine strike later on saw him create a club record by having scored in each of his first four appearances. By the end, we'd even seen passages of first-time passing reminiscent of the old Luton. A sloppy pair of goals were conceded, but you can't have everything.

Buckle focused his early training sessions on rehearsal of set plays, and it was reported that a couple of players didn't think much of this and failed to take it seriously; Buckle applied zero tolerance by dropping the offenders from his plans completely, and they were gone within a few weeks. He didn't have the 'hard man' looks of his predecessor, but Buckle was clearly no shrinking violet.

Fighting spirit was needed following the woeful recent away performances – and Buckle seemed to have generated some. At Alfreton at the end of the week there was a good attitude, and although it ended as a rather dour 0-0, Luton were the only likely winners, Gray hitting a post and sub Boucaud having a header cleared off the line. The 'new manager effect' was in evidence, and at home to Ebbsfleet three nights on, we enjoyed some of the best attacking football of the campaign in a 3-0 success. Fleetwood snapped a pair of cracking goals, either side of the interval, and the icing on the cake was McAllister's first for the club in his tenth appearance. Roars of collective relief greeted him making the most of a goalkeeping howler. It all left us one place outside the play-off zone, two points adrift, but with a game in hand. We still had a fighting chance and smiles were returning to the faces.

Conveniently, the team one place above us – Kidderminster – came to Kenilworth Road next, and with matches fast running out it was clear the winner of this tussle would take a giant step towards the play-offs. The biggest crowd of the season so far (8,415) was in fine voice and a tense and intriguing contest was decided when Tyler raced out of goal and sent a brilliant pass to the feet of Willmott, who produced an expert piece of finishing that brought the house down. Ecstatic Willmott said later, 'The atmosphere was unbelievable. You always wonder what it would be like to score a winner, and when that goal went in it was mental. I could feel my legs turning to jelly.' Buckle called the crowd's contribution 'staggering', and added, 'After we scored and were going for a second the noise levels were absolutely unbelievable. I told the players not to be afraid of it, but to embrace it.' He praised the team for quickly taking on board new information he'd passed on in the fortnight since becoming manager.

Into the final week of the season and the improvement meant Luton now needed just two points from the final two games to be certain of a play-off place – away at Gateshead, and then at Fleetwood, already confirmed as champions. It proved a grim midweek affair at the under-populated Gateshead athletics stadium, and the goalless draw looked a decent result after Tyler made a wonderful save to prevent a Taylor own goal, and The Heed hit a post in the last minute. It was all down to the wire on the last day. We headed to the final game at Fleetwood, needing one point to be certain of progress, but knowing that if Kidderminster failed to beat Mansfield that would do the job for us.

Fleetwood, skippered by big Steve McNulty, had clinched the Conference title some time earlier after an unbeaten run of twenty-nine games. It meant they had little to play for against Luton, and, encouragingly, had taken their foot off the pedal a week earlier when losing their unbeaten run at Cambridge. It seemed an opportune time to be facing the Cod Army in their own backyard. To help persuade them to take things easy, we even applauded them on the pitch with a guard of honour.

Luton got off to a great start when McAllister's high cross to the far post was deflected in off Pond's head after just 8 minutes. Victory was ultimately sealed on 69 minutes when great work by Willmott was finished by Gray right in front of the jubilant away fans. In the dying moments, the league programme almost ended with a wonder goal, Osano racing from halfway on a mazy slalom run, beating five defenders, before unluckily seeing his shot hit the 'keeper's outstretched foot. News filtered through that Kidderminster had lost 3-0 to Mansfield so all was well anyway. Mission accomplished, for now. The Luton fan dressed in a one-piece orange-skin suit did a wild dance for the television cameras and we were home and dry and into the dreaded play-offs for a third successive season.

May 2012: One of Wembley's Quickest Goals

Thankfully, this year's play-offs culminated at Wembley Stadium, unlike twelve months earlier. It was certainly the most exciting way to get promoted, although few seem to welcome the nail-biting tension and pressure of a two-legged semi-final. History showed that the clubs who triumph in these circumstances tend to be those who made a late run and squeezed into contention by the skin of their teeth, and not the better-placed clubs who only just missed out on automatic promotion. So that's a good omen for Luton, as opponents Wrexham finished runners-up on ninety-eight points, a massive nineteen ahead of us. Andy Morrell's men went into the play-offs feeling grumpy and hard done by, whereas we were pleased and relieved to have made it. So who would be in the best frame of mind to rise to the challenge?

Luton's record in two-legged semi-finals was mixed. Three wins and three losses sprung immediately to mind: we triumphed over two legs against Oxford and West Ham in the 1988 and 1989 League Cups, and the previous year had walloped Wrexham in a double header. On the other hand, there were painful memories of Crewe, York and Mansfield edging us out in two-legged semis by narrow margins. The vibes seemed promising. Buckle reported that the players were enjoying training and called the first leg at home to Wrexham the biggest occasion of his management career. The atmosphere was electric as more than 9,000 squeezed into Kenilworth Road on a balmy Thursday evening, hoping for a repeat of last season's first leg hammering of the Red Dragons.

The dream start we had wished for was granted, Luton creating two magnificent goals before the half-hour mark. Fleetwood and Gray combined in two counter-attacks, their pace, precision passing and clinical finishing worthy of a far bigger stage than 'Division Five'.

Wrexham gathered themselves and applied heavy pressure after the restart, but without success, while at the other end it was almost three when a Kovács effort was cleared off the line. And so we headed to North Wales four days later on Bank Holiday Monday, armed with a 2-0 lead and a hefty, noisy following. Six clean sheets in a row and seven games without defeat meant it had been quite a turnaround since Buckle's arrival less than a month earlier.

The two semi-final second legs were scheduled to be screened one after the other on live television, but it seemed nobody expected extra time would be required in the first game between Mansfield and York. The consequence was Luton and Wrexham facing a long delay to kick-off at the Racecourse. That was a new one. Welcome to the Conference. Once finally underway, the air was thick with tension as we scrapped hard to keep the eager home side at bay. There was huge relief after 25 minutes when Creighton crudely brought down Lawless, and Pilkington, cool as a cucumber, converted the spot-kick for a 3-0 aggregate lead.

For a while, Wrexham looked flat and beaten, but got a second wind after winger Cieslewicz came off the bench to terrorise our left flank, supported by the experienced Little. They equalised just past the hour when the sub's header from a corner drifted in at a far post, mysteriously unguarded by any Luton players. With the crowd roaring them forward, they snatched another through Morrell 13 minutes from time, a scrambled and disputed affair that reduced Luton's aggregate lead to just one goal, ratcheting the tension to a new high. We employed the time-wasting tactics we see so often from opponents at Kenilworth Road, and somehow held firm through a hectic 7 minutes of added time to spark great scenes of celebration. The whistle signalled a dejected collapse to the turf by deflated Wrexham players, but they were soon upright again when a pitch invasion by home fans got underway.

So. Another year, another final, and yet another battle with the men of York City. The big game on Sunday 20 May was at the revamped Wembley Stadium. In the stands, at least, it would prove a very one-sided affair, with around 30,000 Luton fans easily outshouting the modest 7,000 or so representing the Minstermen. Sadly, this dominance didn't spread to the field. Despite the team's improvements of recent weeks, for the fourth time in eight visits to the national stadium, Luton fans saw their team fail to rise to the occasion – albeit seriously hampered on this day by one particular slice of downright bad luck. At big games here in 1959 (Nottingham Forest), 1988 (Reading) and 1994 (Chelsea), Luton 'failed to turn up', as the saying goes, and apart from the odd flicker of excitement, it happened again in 2012.

Victory would complete a memorable nine days for York, having already won the FA Trophy, gained planning permission for a new ground and now regaining the League status that was lost in 2004. But they had to overcome a truly remarkable start by Luton, Willmott weaving in from the left and releasing Gray to guide a carefully placed low shot in via the far post. Jubilation after just 72 seconds. But instead of building on this incredible start, Luton simply never got going, and fluency was not achieved. By the half-hour point, York clawed back level though a powerful Chambers finish, and began to look the more likely winners. Shortly after the interval, a throw found Parslow, who nodded on towards Blair, clearly two or three yards offside as he tucked the ball past Tyler. It happened quickly, but was so blatant there could be no excuse for the flag not being raised. Buckle would say later, 'If it had been nip and tuck, I would agree with giving it to the striker. But this was so far offside, it was so wrong. It was crystal clear and that cost us dearly.' In the afterglow of victory, even Blair admitted he'd been lucky.

A week earlier, Sergio Aguero had won the Premiership for Manchester City in the dying seconds of the final match – and that sort of drama was what we needed now from weary Luton. Sadly, it was never on the cards, for they simply couldn't find a way through stubborn opposition, despite totting up twenty-one shots on goal, twice as many as York. Thus a sixth successive season at Luton ended in gut-wrenching failure. But what other club would send 30,000 to Wembley at the tail end of such a period? The punishment for those sins by our management of yesteryear continued, and a fourth year of non-League football was all we had to look forward to over the subsequent summer. This writer had been following Luton for more than thirty-five years by now, so was well used to putting on a brave face, but there are certain occasions when a fellow is quite entitled to act like a grumpy old git. Losing to an offside goal at Wembley is most definitely one of them.

To try and flush away the misery, I tried blogging my top five whinges about our disastrous day in the London Borough of Brent. It seemed like a coping mechanism worth trying. Certainly cheaper and healthier than alcohol anyway. They came out as follows: (1) the wretched weather – it was far too cold, overcast and windy. Wembley finals are supposed to be played in intense heat, bright sunshine and strength-sapping humidity; (2) the rip-offs – a small bottle of water inside Wembley cost £2.20. And they insisted on pouring it into a plastic beaker before handing it over. Why? Who on earth would pay £2.20 for water and then chuck it at somebody else? (3) the rubbish match programme – Dan Gleeson was chosen as Luton's 'one to watch' when he hadn't started a game since January, and they had Danny Crow on the front cover, even though he hadn't featured in the last ten games; (4) The pre-match entertainment – somebody in a suit sang at incredibly high volume into Wembley's powerful PA system, and then excitedly introduced a young woman described as a South Korean soprano, even though she was from the USA. What was all that about? (5) my failure to have a bet – I was asked before kick-off who would be first scorer. Of course I replied Andre Gray, who promptly proved me right after just 72 seconds. But did I back my own judgement at the BetFred kiosk? No.

Luton fans could have drummed up hundreds of reasons for feeling down and bruised as we dragged our wrung-out carcasses away from Wembley that day. But top of the list had to be that offside winning goal. Those who checked it out on YouTube later found it had been even more offside than we first thought. A nearly forgivable mistake by the officials quickly grew into a major blunder. It meant our punishment had been prolonged to a minimum four years in the Conference.

There was probably only one Luton man who could raise a smile at this point, and that was club director David Wilkinson. After the match he was stopped in central London by a traffic cop, who warned him that his inflammatory behaviour was likely to cause a public nuisance. David's shock turned to laughter when the officer said all charges would be dropped if he replaced his Luton car sticker with a Watford one. Crikey – a Hornet with a sense of humour? This really had been a strange season.

4

2012/13 Season

August 2012:
Buckle Up – He's Hell-Bent on Promotion!

Keith Keane, Luton through and through, wearer of the shirt 284 times in four different divisions, had had enough. The prospect of a fourth season outside the Football League was trumped by overtures from Preston North End, and the boy was away. He'd be sorely missed, as would skipper and defensive rock George Pilkington, who decided to head north to join Mansfield. But we could rest easy in our beds. The incoming summer signings by Buckle looked, on paper at least, to be more than adequate replacements. There was Stevenage captain Ronnie Henry, Gillingham pair Danny Spiller and Garry Richards, Wycombe forward Scott Rendell, Gateshead striker Jon Shaw, Matt Robinson from Leicester, Torquay's Lathaniel Rowe-Turner and Brighton's Yaser Kasim on loan. These looked the type of signings that most Conference clubs could only dream about.

Well over 4,000 season tickets were sold, anticipation was as keen as ever, and we were once again the bookies' favourites for promotion. A feel-good factor had swept the nation thanks to the London 2012 Olympics, and Luton fans responded by turning up to preseason friendlies in unfeasibly high numbers. We had narrowly failed to escape three times now, but nobody was starting to feel at home at Conference level as far as I could see. And Buckle and his henchmen seemed in no doubt over expectation levels around these parts: 'I'm hell bent on promotion,' he reassured us.

Of course, the reality check came rudely early. This was Luton after all. After 35 minutes of the opening game, we were playing like a group of strangers and were 0-2 down at home to humble Gateshead. A double substitution was made at half-time, but more than an hour passed before the depression slowly settling over Kenilworth Road was lifted, Shaw poking home a debut goal. Ten minutes later, unmarked Fleetwood rifled an equaliser. Only a point was gained, but at least we ended the game with

Above: 1. Asa Hall (*left*) fires Luton's third goal in a 3-0 win over Grays Athletic. (*Image courtesy of Luton News*)

Below: 2. Jake Howells flicks in Luton's seventh first-half goal in an 8-0 win over Hayes & Yeading. (*Image courtesy of Luton News*)

Above: 3. Tom Craddock grabs the second goal in a 4-0 win over Salisbury City. (*Image courtesy of Luton News*)

Below: 4. Manager Richard Money acknowledges fans on one of his happier days at Luton. (*Image courtesy of Luton News*)

5. Asa Hall is swamped by teammates after a goal against Tamworth. (*Image courtesy of Luton News*)

6. Matthew Barnes-Homer in action in the snow at Eastbourne. (*Image courtesy of Luton News*)

Left: 7. Skipper Kevin Nicholls urges more effort against Chester. (*Image courtesy of Luton News*)

Below: 8. The show must go on … the snow must go off! (*Image courtesy of Luton News*)

9. One-way traffic ... Luton's best win of the Conference era, 8-0 against Hayes & Yeading. (*Image courtesy of Luton News*)

10. Craddock gets a cross over during a 2-2 draw against Cambridge United. (*Image courtesy of Luton News*)

Above: 11. Keith Keane played in three divisions of the League for Luton even before the Conference era. (*Image courtesy of Luton News*)

Below: 12. Goalscorer Robbie Willmott (No. 11) is congratulated by Jason Walker (23) and Jake Howells. (*Image courtesy of Luton News*)

13. Experienced veteran Kevin Gallen has a shot on goal in a 0-0 draw with Altrincham. (*Image courtesy of Luton News*)

14. Manager Paul Buckle, whose stint in charge was filled with highs and lows. (*Author's image*)

15. Andre Gray, a bargain at £30,000, celebrates scoring on his debut, a 1-1 draw with Grimsby. (*Image courtesy of Luton News*)

Above left: 16. Even Santa Claus is a Luton supporter! (*Author's image*)

Above right: 17. Sell-out at Wembley Stadium? Not bad for a Conference club! (*Author's image*)

18. Luton fans get their message across at Wembley Stadium. (*Author's image*)

19. Pre-match fun and games prior to the play-off final against York City at Wembley. (*Author's image*)

20. Manager John Still (*left*) and managing director Gary Sweet. (*Image courtesy of Luton News*)

Above: 21. Paul Benson crashes home a last-minute goal in a 3-0 win over Chester. (*Image courtesy of Luton News*)

Below: 22. John Still likes to include supporters in the post-match 'huddle'. (*Image courtesy of Luton News*)

23. Fans Dannii and Mary Scarlino crack open five-year-old champagne the night the title is clinched. (*Image courtesy of M. Scarlino*)

24. Manager John Still mingles with fans after the 2-1 win at Welling. (*Author's image*)

25. Players and staff gather in the main stand at Welling the week the title was won. (*Author's image*)

26. A supporter breaks ranks to congratulate manager John Still on the title win. (*Author's image*)

27. 'We are the champions' ... the players sing along with the fans after beating Forest Green 4-1. (*Author's image*)

Above: 28. Thousands flood the pitch after the final home game of the glorious 2013/14 season. (*Author's image*)

Right: 29. Relief and joy in equal measure ... Luton are back in the League and the party is underway. (*Author's image*)

30. After the presentations, the players have fun with mascot Happy Harry's detachable head! (*Image courtesy of Josie Kingston*)

31. Midfielder Cameron McGeehan mingles with admirers after the trophy and medals are presented. (*Author's image*)

32. All set for the town centre parade in May 2014. All we need now is the players! (*Author's image*)

33. The champions' bus arrives in a packed St George's Square in central Luton. (*Image courtesy of Luton News*)

34. Manager John Still acknowledges the crowds after the open-topped bus arrives at the town hall. (*Author's image*)

35. Thirty-goal Andre Gray lifts the Conference trophy on stage in St George's Square. (*Image courtesy of Luton News*)

Above: 36. An estimated 12,000 pack into the town centre to hail the new champions. (*Image courtesy of Luton News*)

Below: 37. Another campaign is over ... one fan's farewell message is loud and clear. (*Author's image*)

forward momentum, and this would be carried over to Kidderminster three days later.

This time it was Luton who cruised into a two-goal lead by the half-hour mark, both well-taken Fleetwood efforts. No further dramas, job done. A visit to Hyde United's sparsely populated little ground in the Greater Manchester suburbs was next, and saw Luton fans accompanied by former star midfielder Alan West, who was born and bred in Hyde. Shockingly, he revealed on live television at half-time that he was actually rooting for the town of his birth tonight, but at least Mrs West was firmly with the Hatters. Blinkhorn put the home side ahead, but in the final 20 minutes or so our efforts bore fruit via two magnificent goals, a long-range effort from youngster O'Donnell and a counter-attack of lightning pace finished by Fleetwood.

We looked good going forward at home to AFC Telford a week later, but did everything but score. St Aimie's first-half headed goal proved the winner, Town hitting the bar and having an effort cleared off the line in a dramatic and bad-tempered finale. Henry and Telford's Preston were red carded after an off-the-ball tussle, and visiting sub Reid departed after just 69 seconds on the pitch. It was the Bucks' first away win in a year, and Luton's first league defeat since Buckle arrived. There was plenty of fallout after the final whistle, both clubs were charged by the FA for not controlling their players, and Shaw was hit by a three-match ban for violent conduct not spotted by the referee. Languishing at ninth in the table was not a pretty sight for Luton fans and 1,245 of us headed over the QE2 Bridge into Kent, demanding a Bank Holiday return to winning ways at Ebbsfleet two days later. Outnumbering home fans by two to one, we got our fifteen quid's worth when Rendell and Fleetwood combined nicely to score a goal apiece in the early stages. Fleetwood fired his sixth of the season later on before an Elder header saw it end up at 1-3.

September 2012: Horror Show on Humberside

Luton supporters can be hard to please, and the 100 per cent away record was not getting too many of us excited due to the simultaneous failure to win at home in August. The visit of Macclesfield became a 'must win' affair if we were to prevent Newport (five wins out of five) streaking out of reach at the top of the table. Injuries and suspension meant young loanee centre-half Connor Essam from Gillingham went straight into our starting line-up, unlike his erstwhile Priestfield colleagues Spiller and Richards, who still hadn't kicked a ball since arrival due to injury. The Silkmen, above us in the table, were put to the sword in fine style, Howells and Gray netting early on. A minor wobble occurred when it was pulled back to 2-1 and Barnes-Homer then struck our crossbar, but Rendell and Fleetwood pounced in the latter stages to make it 4-1 and ease any lingering tension.

The good vibes continued into the following Tuesday with another entertaining victory, Cambridge United were sent back up the A505 with a flea in their ear after daring to take the lead at Kenilworth Road. Wellard lived up to his name with a fiercely struck shot into the roof of Tyler's net. Parity came when Kovács buried a brave header, followed after the interval by a cool Gray finish and a curler from forgottten man Beckwith. McAuley headed the Us second 2 minutes from the end to get the worry beads rattling, but the final 3-2 scoreline flattered the visitors a little. Forest Green also won well that night to become the division's new leaders, with Luton in second just a point behind.

It had been a hectic schedule, and the eighth game in twenty-eight days, away at Alfreton, produced the least palatable performance thus far, outshining the tantrums with Telford and leading to a public apology to the fans from Buckle. Falling behind in the second minute on a scorching hot late summer afternoon, Luton never recovered and the 3-0 end result matched our worst defeat as a Conference club. Loanee Jake Robinson debuted but made little impact at the Impact Arena. The apologetic Buckle was facing trouble on all fronts it seemed, for a few days later squad member Newman Carney had his contract terminated for missing training sessions. Buckle then had to be satisfied with just a point when Wrexham came to town, no goals but plenty of fire and brimstone in a tense contest between two evenly matched promotion-chasers.

Television coverage dictated our trip to Grimsby be played on a Friday evening, which had serious consequences for one coachload of Luton fans. During their 320-mile round trip they got caught up in major traffic congestion, only arriving at Blundell Park in time to see the start of the second half. But their nightmare journey was nothing compared to the horror show in Luton's defence, which by this point had been breached three times. Centre-backs Kovács and Beckwith had an awful night, and their misfortune would lead to Buckle signing Simon Ainge on loan to stiffen things up. We fell 4-0 behind on 70 minutes, survived more near misses and then pulled one back through Rendell before this grimmest of 90 minutes came thankfully to a close. This month had got off to a great start, but suddenly Buckle appeared to be facing a mini-crisis after two thumping defeats.

There were all manner of team changes, including a revamped back four, as we headed to Tamworth to get things back on track. This was the ground where Richard Money went into meltdown two years ago, and when Luton went in at half-time a goal behind, Buckle looked like he might be about to follow suit. In atrocious wind and rain, a free header had hit our net and when the hour mark approached with Luton still behind, Buckle took the most drastic action open to him, sending on three subs together. Within minutes he was hailed a tactical genius, for two of the new faces (Kasim and Fleetwood) turned the game on its head by shooting us into the lead. By the end we could have had more, and the sheer determination shown in the final half-hour produced a tangible sense of togetherness and mutual admiration between management, players and 390 travelling fans. All a far cry from August 2010, when Money left this pitch ranting and raving and gesticulating at his own supporters.

For the first time in six games, we opened the scoring when mid-table Southport were the visitors. Fleetwood side-footed home in the 4th minute, and we looked to be cruising until Parry levelled on the stroke of half-time. This development led to a tongue-lashing for the players and an improved second-half showing. Rendell stretched to knock home a low O'Donnell cross and then converted the team's first penalty of the season after Fleetwood was tripped. It was confidently netted, using a cute stop-start run-up, and gave hope that maybe we'd finally found ourselves a penalty expert for the foreseeable future.

October 2012: 'My Strangest Match of All'

Memories of the recent Grimsby debacle were swept away during a return visit across the Fens to Sincil Bank, where we took all three points from Lincoln, holding on brilliantly in the latter stages as the home side went hell for leather for an equaliser. I don't recall spotting a kitchen sink in our goalmouth, but our defenders reckoned it was definitely among the things thrown at them before the whistle finally went. This third successive win lifted us back into the play-off zone and came partly courtesy of a stroke of luck when Imps 'keeper Farman punched a Gray cross into his own net. A half-time double substitution paid off when Shaw headed us further in front, the first goal in twelve games from a striker of whom so much was expected. A spectacular strike by Taylor hauled the home side back into the game, but superb defending prevented further damage and the large away contingent was able to celebrate long and hard in this cathedral city.

Behind the scenes there was talk of the club purchasing the freehold of the stadium back from the local council, who took ownership of our much-maligned but much-loved little home more than twenty years ago, when Tory MP David Evans was in charge here. If nothing else, this highlighted the fact the club was not necessarily hell-bent on moving to a new ground, although we were told from the boardroom that no definitive decisions on this subject had yet been made. One way or another, the Hatters had been looking at the possibility of moving for half a century now, so the news of talks with the council caused very little fuss among the fan base. We knew a move had to happen someday soon, but I suspected many would be extremely sad to walk out of our atmospheric, if old-fashioned, current address for the last time.

It's a ground that has seen just about everything over the decades, but one club we never dreamed would be a regular visitor was little Braintree Town. As recently as the late 1990s, they were way down the pyramid in the Ryman Isthmian Third Division, but were now flourishing under the no-nonsense leadership of Alan Devonshire, and were certainly no pushover. Their Tuesday night visit to Kenilworth Road turned into what Buckle called 'the strangest football match I've ever been involved in'. Luton dominated possession and created many openings, but with barely 30 minutes on the clock, we found ourselves two goals and a man down. Fleetwood picked up two highly controversial yellow cards, one for allegedly diving. The visitors mercilessly took their limited chances with surprising panache, while countless opportunities were spurned at the other end. Then Ainge's header and a fine Walker strike, 45 seconds after coming on, provided real hope that sanity would be restored. However, the resolute Essex boys hung on to their 3-2 lead, leaving everyone in orange, both on and off the pitch, shaking their heads in disbelief at the outcome. It was a night when the world was against us, reflected skipper Henry.

The massive frustration only began to dissipate in the very final stages of the next game, at home to Nuneaton, a team that didn't even have enough players to fill their subs bench. Just as we were thinking more crucial points were slipping away, Lawless snapped up a brace in the final 5 minutes, his first a real beauty that swerved in from 25 yards. During the subsequent two-week break from league action, Buckle did a deal with Macclesfield, giving them Kissock (the poor man's Messi) in exchange for enigmatic Guinea-Bissau international Arnaud Mendy (the poor man's YaYa Toure). The new boy debuted the following day as we beat Cambridge United 2-0 at the Abbey in the FA Cup fourth qualifying round.

Things were generally looking a little brighter again after our seventh away win of the season was chalked up even before the end of October. It was an encouragingly gritty 2-1 success at Forest Green, where we came from behind to win. Fleetwood curled a smart equaliser and Rendell netted a last-minute penalty winner.

November 2012: A Month Best Forgotten

Nuneaton returned to Kenilworth Road just three weeks after their league visit, determined to stifle Luton again and win themselves an FA Cup first round replay. They managed it, and almost pulled off a shock win, leading for 64 minutes before Rendell headed an equaliser. Two days later, Buckle stiffened his midfield with the acquisition of tough-tackling Jonathan Smith from York, a player he'd tried to purchase from Swindon only a few months earlier. Smith debuted in a one-sided affair at Hereford, where Luton again failed to capitalise on good possession and chances, and came up against a goalkeeper in inspired form. We forced twelve corners and had twenty goal attempts, compared to one and six by Hereford, but the only stat that really mattered was McQuilkin netting the Bulls' winner shortly before the hour mark. It left Town third in the table, four points adrift of leaders Newport.

Even less palatable than the Edgar Street defeat was a 0-2 reverse at home to newly promoted Dartford four days later. We had no divine right to beat clubs of the stature of Braintree and Dartford, of course, but losing to part-timers is an embarrassment all the same, especially for the long-standing supporters like this writer. After Noble's early free-kick sailed past everyone to open the scoring, Bonner got clear to increase the Darts' lead before half-time. The jeers rang out from home fans, the players' heads went down and we rarely looked like mounting a serious comeback, despite Gray striking the crossbar. We were dropping far too many points at home, and even a 2-0 FA Cup replay win at Nuneaton failed to alter the opinion of most fans that we simply didn't have the consistency to challenge seriously for the one automatic promotion place. The title race looked far more open this year than for some time, yet nobody seemed to want to take advantage, including Luton.

There was no such thing as an easy game in this league, or so the managers were fond of saying, and they certainly don't come much tougher at this level than a trip to Field Mill, Mansfield. The task became even harder when long-throw expert Geohaghon hurled one of his missiles into our box and Hutchinson headed the Stags into an early lead. It took two pieces of fine finishing by Gray to turn things around, only for another set-piece goal – five minutes from the end – to restrict us to a single point at 2-2. Another case of points dropped, and there was no immediate chance to put things right, because we now faced the oddity of three cup ties in eight days – and all were against the same opposition. Dorchester Town, from a division below, held us 2-2 in the first round of the FA Trophy at the Avenue Stadium, meaning the sides had to replay at Kenilworth Road as well as fit in an FA Cup second-round tie in the same week. No disrespect intended towards The Magpies, but Luton fans felt a tad underwhelmed by all this.

December 2012: Now is the Winter of Our Discontent

Progress was made in both cups against Dorchester; 2-1 in the FA Cup, which set up a third round tie at home to Wolves; and a less welcomed 3-1 win in the FA Trophy. Fringe players got some first team action, but many regular fans gave these games a miss, only 897 watching the Trophy replay, Luton's lowest-ever gate for any competitive first team game. Just sixteen hardy souls were seen rattling around in the away enclosure that Tuesday night.

It had been a while since a comfortable home win, so a 3-0 triumph over a dogged Alfreton outfit was just what the doctor ordered. Nicky Law's men tried everything, including wasting time in the first half, to frustrate and break our rhythm. But their pesky game plan went to pieces when a 5-minute blitz saw us score three times just after the break. O'Donnell, Smith and Gray were on target, the latter's effort a peach of a volley from Henry's cross.

Three days later came a midweek challenge of an altogether different variety, a fixture at league leaders Newport. With Kovács suspended and loanee Smith recalled by his parent club, this was always likely to be a tough and very cold night's work on a pitch that only narrowly passed two pre-match inspections. Old friend and keen Twitter exponent O'Connor opened the scoring against his former club, but a quick-fire equaliser from Gray warmed the cockles of the 177 brave travelling fans. The home side generally looked more purposeful in the miserable conditions, and by half-time had forged a decisive 3-1 lead. Shaw netted on 61 minutes to give us hope, but the lively Jolley and Sandell responded with further goals and County were good value for their 5-2 success. It was the first time Luton had conceded five for almost four years, and the inevitable consequence was a fair number of fans making it known they wanted Buckle replaced. Yes, already. We were still fifth but, having now lost seven of twenty-one league games, were slipping out of contention for the title, so the discontent was hardly surprising.

A 2-1 win four days later over little Matlock in the FA Trophy didn't bring too much comfort, and it looked like a long, hard winter was ahead. An FA Cup visit by Wolves was something to look forward to, but most fans would probably swap that for half-a-dozen more league points. Nevertheless, a good Boxing Day crowd of nearly 7,000 turned out for the visit of mid-table Woking. Two first-half goals was their reward, Kovács heading in from a corner and Shaw smashing home after good work by Gray. McNerny nipped in to halve the lead with 20 minutes left, but any fears of letting this one slip disappeared when Lawless was bundled over and Rendell netted a precise penalty. The chance to bag a further three points over the holiday period disappeared when the home match with Ebbsfleet was called off due to a soggy pitch a mere 20 minutes before kick-off time, due to a soggy pitch. Thousands of fans were already in the ground or in the vicinity by then, and their anger was understandable, particularly as the skies were clearing and the sun came out shortly afterwards.

January 2013: 'New Scenery, New Noise'

Going into the new year with seven defeats already on the board, it was clear there was little margin for error in the weeks ahead as we hit the season's halfway mark. However, our recent habit of dominating games for long periods but failing to win continued in the return game with Woking. Knott swept The Cards into an early lead, but a superb effort from Gray deservedly levelled matters. At 1-1, Shaw twice struck wood before we crumbled infuriatingly to two late goals, both of which looked preventable. The no-nonsense ball-winner Smith had been recaptured from York at a cost of £50,000, and we looked like we needed the stuff he was made of, and plenty of it. He and the rest of the squad were made to sit down by Buckle and watch the entire Woking game on DVD in an attempt to analyse where our problems lay. Smith went straight into the starting line-up for the much-anticipated Cup showdown with Championship strugglers Wolves.

Ah, the FA Cup third round ... forget all the Conference torment, for here was the first Saturday of the year and one of the top dates on the English football calendar. And what an atmosphere at the Kenny, almost 10,000 inside and the away end packed to the gills for the first time in ages. The television cameras were here hoping for a giant-killing, and even Sky's *Soccer AM* resident madman Franky Fryer filmed a lengthy segment in and around the ground, getting so excited at one point that he actually dislocated his shoulder. There was an altogether different whiff in the air from a Conference game. Perhaps it was the whiff of nostalgia for us old 'uns; kids and newbies who started coming in the last five or six years would have seen nothing like this before.

Gray, rejected by Wolves as a junior, went close twice against a side that didn't look up for this battle. Relegated from the Premiership six months earlier, they were prime giant-killing fodder, on a poor run lately amid talk that manager Stale Solbakken was on borrowed time. Luton's big moment came just 47 seconds after the restart, a poor clearance from ex-Hatter Foley finding its way via Shaw to Lawless, who volleyed home a beauty from the edge of the box. 'Keeper Ikeme stood no chance. The roar could be heard in Milton Keynes, reckoned one Town official, and he might just have been right. No further scoring in a raucous atmosphere, and we clung ferociously to 1-0 through a mega 9 minutes of added time, caused largely by a nasty facial injury to O'Donnell. For Luton it was time to bask in the limelight, with the likes of Scotland boss Gordon Strachan telling ITV viewers Kenilworth Road was 'a terrific place to play football on days like this'. The icing on the cake came in the draw for round four, when we were handed a tie at Premiership Norwich. For Wolves it was meltdown time, their embarrassment proving the final straw for Solbakken, who was shown the door without delay.

The big question was whether we could take this sort of form and attitude into subsequent league games. The answer was a resounding affirmative when Barrow came to town just three evenings later and suffered a right old larruping. The pacy Scott Neilson, whose quiet debut at Woking went almost unnoticed, opened the scoring after 82 seconds, a Kovács header doubling the lead. The one-way traffic continued and Shaw then collected a 35-minute hat-trick, followed by Gray going clear to complete a comprehensive 6-1 mauling. We now had three games in hand and were eight points behind leaders Wrexham, but poor Barrow were looking relegation certainties.

To add to the mounting fixture congestion we faced, two Saturdays went by without league fixtures, the first when we progressed in the FA Trophy with a routine 2-0 disposal of Skelmersdale, the second due to freezing weather blanketing the UK. A midweek tussle at relegation-threatened AFC Telford went ahead though, with three points looking a must. But as is the way of this league, lower-ranked clubs often provided the stiffest opposition, and there was little to choose between the teams in a goalless bore. Hard-working Telford hit a post and Shaw blazed Luton's best chance over. We slipped back out of the top five places, and it was getting seriously worrying that this highly unacceptable situation was being masked by all the fuss surrounding the FA Cup run.

We had toppled Wolves, fifty-nine places ahead of us in the league ladder, but at Carrow Road, Norwich, the contest was between thirteenth and ninety-eighth – a massive gap of eighty-five places in the great scheme of things. But it was a good time to be playing the Canaries, who hadn't won for more than a month, and a week earlier had conceded five to Liverpool. Chris Hughton juggled his team around to face Luton, whereas Buckle naturally went for his strongest possible options. No non-League side had ever beaten a Premiership outfit on their own turf, but we fancied our chances of doing well as long as there were no early setbacks. What ensued was the stuff of dreams, not only making club history, but getting us splashed across the front and back of national newspapers and capturing the imagination of an underdog-loving nation. It proved an intriguing contest, evenly balanced throughout with little hint of the gulf between the sides. Tyler, a Norwich reject in his youth, had to make a couple of top-class saves, but we looked far more assured and organised than we often did against the Conference scufflers.

'New scenery, new noise', as the great French poet Rimbaud wrote, and the fantastic support from 4,000 Lutonians on one side of Carrow Road was relentless. Goalscoring opportunities were at a premium at both ends, and the tie remained goalless as the clock ticked towards the final 15 minutes. Then came the managerial master stroke, what would surely go down as Buckle's finest moment as a Luton employee – he made three attacking substitutions. The sheer cheek of it. Shouldn't little Luton have shown more respect and retreated to protect what they'd got? Buckle was having none of that and threw on pacy youngster O'Donnell to run the left flank, replacing the more experienced Mendy. Then he replaced reliable workhorse Shaw with the more mercurial Rendell, who was itching to get on because of various personal East Anglian connections. Finally, Buckle opted for nimble-witted Fleetwood in place of sprinter Gray. Eighty minutes were on the clock when we saw instant results: Fleetwood picked up a headed clearance in midfield, darted into space and sprayed a lovely ball through to the accelerating O'Donnell, who was rocketing down the left. The little man reached the line, cut in and pulled back a perfect ball for the advancing Rendell, who got there first to flick it into the roof of the net. The 4,000 away fans could hardly have had a better view and the noise was incredible. It would sound good on television later, but as one fan said, you needed to be there to really appreciate the sheer intensity. Even Bernard Matthews' nearby turkeys must have got goosebumps.

The goal had the effect of a mouse nipping the backside of a lazy cat. It shook Norwich out of their lethargy and meant Luton had to resist a yellow tide for the last 13 minutes. But we survived and the final whistle signalled prolonged mayhem, with even home fans sportingly clapping along in grudging admiration. As many in Luton colours would point out, this was not a giant-killing in the truest sense, for Norwich were a top-flight side punching above their weight and Luton's lowly status was false. Nevertheless we had created history by becoming the first non-Leaguers to overturn a Premiership side away from home, and the first on any ground since Sutton beat Coventry twenty-four years earlier. After all the trouble and strife of the depressing Conference, this was truly a day to savour.

Blogger David Mosque summed up the Luton paradox:

Here's a club that labours in the mud against Woking, gets out-muscled by Braintree and implodes against Dartford, yet keeps clean sheets against teams scores of places above. If ever a club was 'to the Manor Born' it's us isn't it? We are the Audrey fforbes-Hamiltons of the football world. Forced to live in the gatehouse while the nouveau-riche Richard DeVere wallows in cash in the manor house. We are the aristocrats forced to sell the country mansion and move into a council flat. We are the public schoolboys reduced to attending an inner city comprehensive. It's not nice on the shitty side of the street, but boy we're at home in posh company.

Despite recent trials and tribulations, and all the moaning and groaning, most Luton fans did seem to be keeping the faith about a return to the League. Surely, when promotion did finally come, that crisp day in snowy Norfolk might just be the single match-day that lingered longest in the memory from the non-League years. Through to the last sixteen of the FA Cup we went, but the televised draw the following evening proved somewhat disappointing as we were paired with Millwall. Equally underwhelming was the frankly rather predictable 0-3 defeat a few days later at Grimsby in an FA Trophy quarter-final tie at blustery Blundell Park. Good riddance to that competition, some might say. Mind you, it would only need a couple more Conference setbacks and we could find we were missing out on Wembley on all three fronts.

February 2013: Another One Bites the Dust

Before the transfer window slammed shut, Buckle made a late swoop for little Southend winger David Martin and burly Fleetwood defender and skipper Steve McNulty. They didn't wear suits and bowler hats, but this pair bore a passing resemblance to Laurel and Hardy. Luckily, Big Steve was well used to cheap jibes about his size – football fans are an unforgiving lot – and was actually a talented defender with dozens of appearances for Liverpool reserves on his CV. Fleetwood fans were said to be angry Macca had been allowed to leave by their new manager, the former Hatter Graham Alexander. The new men went straight into Luton's team travelling to Barrow, a trip that could hardly be in starker contrast to the previous week's Cup excitement at Carrow Road.

What a difference a week makes. Holker Street echoed to the sound of just 1,118 spectators, thin sunshine glinting on the empty terrace steps, a million miles away from the noise and intensity of last week. But the chaps had to find inspiration from somewhere otherwise the unthinkable – not qualifying for the play-offs – could become reality. And they got off to a dreadful start. The defence that had proudly remained unbreached on a Premiership ground seven days earlier, succumbed in only the 3rd minute, and it was a real 'head-in-hands' moment for full-back Taylor. A giant punt downfield by the Barrow 'keeper came his way and he attempted a risky cushioned header as it fell from the sky, only succeeding in presenting the ball to Boyes, who lobbed Tyler with ease. On the sidelines, Buckle went ballistic. There were 87 minutes to hit back, but an equaliser failed to arrive, despite much pressure and hard toil. To cap a miserable afternoon, Rowe-Turner was red carded in the dying moments for an off-the-ball misdemeanor. Buckle lashed out publicly at Taylor's match-losing error, calling it 'pathetic'. Frustrated fans readily agreed, but there was nevertheless criticism of Buckle for giving an individual such a public dressing down. The manager responded by recruiting an experienced defender, well-travelled Wayne Thomas, who had spent the previous 18 months playing in Greece.

Promotion-chasing Forest Green came to Kenilworth Road a week later, no doubt buoyed by the prospect of a facing a discontented and ever-changing Luton line-up that had failed to score in three league games, and had apparently taken its collective eye off the ball thanks to the FA Cup run. Encouragingly, well over 6,000 turned out, proving the fans hadn't totally lost faith in our promotion chances yet, and there was a bright start as Gray's mistimed header somehow looped gently into the net. In contrast to the lack of power behind the header, Gray would later smash a penalty towards the centre of the goal, only to see it fly over the bar and towards the top of the stand. This awful miss was one of three calamities, the others an equaliser conceded from another set piece, and the dismissal of Lawless for two yellow cards in quick succession. The game ended all square and even a red card for FGR's ex-Watford forward Bangura failed to cheer us up.

During the midweek, before the FA Cup visit of Millwall, more league points had to be fought over in our first-ever visit to Princes Park, Dartford. It proved a 90-minute slog, Luton struggling to create clear chances despite fielding two wingers, Neilson and Martin, to provide ammo for Gray and Shaw. Gray hit a post, but the home side were tough nuts to crack and netted a winner on 72 minutes through a fine shot from distance by Hayes. Depressingly, this was Luton's tenth defeat of the season, and we were down to seventh and six points off the play-off zone. All was not lost yet, but there was little sign of the mustering the sort of momentum needed to claw our way back upwards. The anti-Buckle brigade were in full voice by now, which is probably not surprising as we were looking less healthy than under his predecessors Harford, Money and Brabin – all of whom were ditched mid-season.

It would have been so typical of Luton to topple Millwall and become the first non-League outfit in history to reach the FA Cup quarter-finals, while simultaneously heading for the club's lowest league finish ever. The Lions, a mid-table Championship outfit, had lost their last four league games, meaning it was a fairly level playing field in terms of recent form. A near sell-out crowd drummed up a good atmosphere, but the buoyant Cup mood was deflated when a slip by Kovács let in Henry to open the scoring early on. Gray and Mendy went close at the other end, but the killer goal came just before the interval when Hulse's overhead kick, surely an intended cross, looped into the far corner. The visitors were too strong in most departments, and the game was dead and buried after N'Guessan forced home the rebound after a Tyler save. Millwall avoided the big guns and were paired with Blackburn in the quarter-final draw, leaving Luton to reflect on what might have been, and a return to the bread and butter of eighteen remaining Conference games.

That return to normality hit home just three days later, with a long away trek to Macclesfield, but pre-match preparations would be thrown into chaos when sensational news broke just a couple of hours before kick-off. The club revealed Buckle had left his post that day for 'genuine personal reasons' that were not related to his job, but which they could not elaborate on. The surprise and mystery surrounding all this meant the rumour mill naturally went into overdrive. Theories and suggestions were put forward by fans – one of which was clearly well informed, for it later turned out to be accurate: Buckle's fiancée, the television football presenter Rebecca Lowe, had landed a high-profile job in the USA and they were leaving together to set up home stateside. Lowe, it transpired, was to head up NBC's Premier League coverage, the couple were to marry in the summer, and, ultimately, Buckle would take the role of technical director at the Met Oval football academy in New York.

In the meantime, inside Luton Town's hotel at Macclesfield, there was a degree of pandemonium as the clock ticked towards kick-off time and the stunned players digested the news they had no manager. As a play-off place was likely to require a tally of around eighty points, Luton went into this game needing around thirty-six points from the remaining eighteen games. It was a tall order and only possible if a complete turnaround of recent form was achieved. One of the most common scenarios for such a turnaround had traditionally been the infusion of new blood into the manager's office, an appointment that would get the pulses racing and signal the start of a 'honeymoon period'. That's all we needed.

With Neilson and his backroom colleagues put in temporary charge, we got off to a lively start at Macc, Gray hitting a post from 25 yards and Shaw sliding the rebound wide. Gray, posing all manner of problems with his pace, then put Luton ahead from close range. Minutes later, he was hauled over outside the box by goalkeeper Taylor as he streaked through looking for a second. The custodian was given a straight red card and the home side was forced to put midfielder Winn in goal. It all boded well for Luton, but ultimately the failure to beat the makeshift 'keeper saw us pay dearly. Second-half pressure from the ten men culminated 15 minutes from the end with an equaliser from 20 yards by Fairhurst, which flew in off a post. We were without a manager, eleven points adrift off the play-offs, five league games without a win and it was nearly March. Woe was us.

The search for a new leader, our fifth in less than four years, got underway, and among the most commonly touted names were former midfielder Steve Robinson and former Stevenage boss Graham Westley, who'd been sacked by Preston a week earlier. Many fans were aghast at any mention of the latter, who, to put it delicately, would be widely regarded as a bad fit at Luton. In the meantime, the first home league game in nearly seven weeks was upon us, play-off chasers Mansfield the visitors. It was certainly no classic, but Town showed a willingness to fight, twice coming from behind. McNulty's foul led to the Stags' opener from the spot, but Rendell equalised calmly when a Smith shot deflected into his path. Just before the break, Daniel put Mansfield back in front, but Gray lashed us level shortly after the restart after another favourable deflection. Toiling desperately for a winner that wouldn't come, we were caught out right at the death when Tyler brilliantly parried Clements' shot, but Meikle converted the rebound to win it 3-2.

Confidence and cohesion were notable by their absence around now, so probably the last thing we needed before a new manager came in and got settled was a trip to the woefully inadequate mud-heap that was Braintree Town's ground. Alan Devonshire's workmanlike outfit would have no sympathy for the wounded animal that was Luton Town. It was a real case of *déjà vu*, for a year earlier Paul Buckle came to Cressing Road to see us lose at Braintree before taking up his duties the next day. Now, on a cold and miserable Tuesday evening, our brand-new boss was also looking on – but not taking charge till the following day. That man – not initially regarded as a contender by speculating fans – was John Still, manager of Dagenham and Redbridge for the past nine years and an old-school campaigner with bags of League Two and Conference experience.

He still must have wondered what he'd let himself in for as he watched Town struggle at Braintree, alongside assistant Terry Harris. It became a contest between two teams of ten when Paine's bad tackle on Mendy saw a red card produced, quickly followed by off-the-ball nonsense leading to the departure of Thomas in only his second game at the heart of our defence. After McNulty was outstripped on the right flank, Marks flicked in the opening goal with his heel and defeat was assured when Davis later headed home at the far post. Caretaker Neilson, probably relieved to be handing over the reins, apologised for an abject evening's work: 'We're all in a real bad place, the players and myself,' he said.

Big John Still is one of those managers who is living proof you don't need an impressive CV as a player to be successful in the manager's chair. He only made one league appearance, his playing days cut cruelly short by injury. His one chance at the big time came in 1967 at Orient, when manager Dick Graham threw a bunch of kids into a struggling team, including seventeen-year-old Still. Also debuting that day for the Os was Barry Fry, signed from Luton, and from that point Still and Fry's careers took strangely similar paths, both going into non-League shortly afterwards as players, then as managers. Both would take charge for spells at Maidstone, Barnet and Peterborough.

Still's first significant steps at Luton would be the capture of two big, strong youngsters – striker Alex Wall from Maidenhead and centre-back Jake Goodman on loan from Millwall. Still had a mountain to climb to get Luton out of the Conference and wisely announced he was not looking at a quick-fix scenario. He was advised by some friends and contacts not to take this job, for it was a potential poisoned chalice, but he clearly couldn't resist the challenge. No doubt he was quickly put in the picture about the huge levels of expectation at Kenilworth Road, the lack of patience of fans when things go wrong, and the PR disasters committed by a certain predecessor called Money, who was nowadays a rival manager at Cambridge United.

March 2013: It's Still – But Will It Also Be Sparkling?

Not so much a new month, more a new era. The good ship Luton Town, with sixty-two-year-old John Still taking command, was in rough waters. Like any huge vessel, turning it around looked a long and arduous task. Things had never been as bad in terms of league position; we were down to tenth (102nd in the pyramid) and in need of a near miracle to reach the play-offs this season. But Still seemed a wise old bird and his first month in charge – which would feature no fewer than eight games – would be largely a matter of assessing what he'd got and what he would need for next season. The optimists among us saw no reason why a play-off push couldn't still be generated, but the stats suggested otherwise, for after thirty-one games we were surely too far adrift, with an unsettled side and a number of injuries. The proliferation of games would also mean limited time on the training field for Still to get his message across and introduce his way of thinking.

After just one training session under the new man, the team chalked up a 1-0 win at relegation-threatened Stockport, and this first away success in the league for over four months returned smiles to many faces. A drab 0-0 at Nuneaton followed, before Hereford came to Luton for the first time in thirty-seven years for a tussle that ended one apiece thanks to a much-improved second-half performance. Martin's cracking late equaliser and some intense spells of pressure helped generate a good atmosphere, and Still was suitably impressed in his first home game. He said he found some of the players inhibited by anxiety in front of the big expectant crowd, and he had to impress on them the need to focus and just 'control the controllables'. It was the first airing for what would soon become his Luton catchphrase.

However, instead of building on that good second-half showing, Luton flopped at home three days later, little Hyde United nicking a shock 2-1 win to end their run of six successive defeats. Still admitted it was a game containing no positives, while skipper Henry called it a disaster. Inevitably, the crowd turned on the team, particularly at the final whistle, and it was only too clear why Still was convinced there would be no quick fix here. Some of the sting was taken out of the barracking when Still kept the team on the pitch at the end for a centre-circle huddle, but it seemed this was normal procedure for him and not just a ploy to avoid confrontation with the boo-boys. Next day, our current league position and the status of the team that beat us led a number of fans to conclude via social media that another new low in Luton's history had been reached. Surely things could only go up from here? Still thought so, and told the media, 'Luton have been out of the Football League for four years and nobody's found the winning formula yet. I've been here two weeks and I'm going to try and find that formula.'

Still brought in Nigerian-born midfielder Solomon Taiwo and the team regained a little pride by holding Wrexham 0-0 at the Racecourse, but seeing the Hatters had dropped to eleventh spot in the next day's papers felt like a real shock to the system. A narrow but welcome 1-0 home triumph over Stockport the following midweek came courtesy of McNulty's first goal for the club, a stooping header to win a one-sided affair. Four days later, there were signs of further improvement when Tamworth came to town amid nasty wintry weather, although the game remained deadlocked at 0-0. Players and backroom staff continued to weave in and out of the club during this period of major transition, one notable signing being Scott Griffiths, a full-back with six seasons of Football League experience to his name. A lively 2-2 draw in a mid-table confrontation at Cambridge saw Luton hang on for a point, Shaw's header and Taiwo's penalty pegging the Us back twice.

The gap between Luton and the play-offs was down to ten points by the end of the month, but with eight games left and form still mixed, the focus was really on next season and beyond. Still had the reassuring air of a manager who could be trusted to do what was necessary, and of someone completely unfazed by the challenge ahead, even though this was the biggest club he had led in thirty-five years as a manager. His calm and disarming manner was very good PR in the circumstances, and his cheerful press conferences were proving a breath of fresh air for the local media.

April 2013: Time to Clear the Decks

The clocks had gone forward, and a long, unhappy Luton Town winter was over. We were all trying very hard to be positive, despite the near-certain prospect of a fifth season out of the Football League. Easter Monday fell on 1 April, and Conference leaders Kidderminster were in town hoping to make April fools of a Luton side that had won only five of its last twenty-three league games. Of the two sides, our visitors looked more like a side going places in the first half; they cruised into a two-goal lead, full of confidence as they set about extending a run of just four defeats from the last thirty-two games. Steve Burr's men had had an extraordinary season, starting the campaign with five successive defeats, following this with five successive draws, and then embarking on the current run to rise from twenty-fourth to first in the table. Luton gave them something to think about as Rendell and Shaw hit their bar, and other chances were spurned before Gray pulled back a solitary consolation goal near the end.

Still's recruitment drive was in full swing and a week later he even missed a Luton game to go scouting. Probably just as well, for in his absence a horror show unfolded, the side going down 5-1 to lowly Gateshead – another strong candidate for 'all-time low' status. It was our heaviest defeat since dropping out of the League. The manager wasn't the only stay-away, for this carnage saw just 382 people rattling around inside Brunton Park, Carlisle (capacity 17,000), which was being used due to Gateshead's stadium being out of action. Nearly half this tiny crowd were hardy perennials from Luton, who made the round trip of more than 500 miles to see a display described by both Still and his captain Henry as 'thoroughly unacceptable'. Neither were at the game, but put themselves through the misery of watching it on DVD a day or two later. Somebody pointed out after Gateshead that it was still mathematically possible for Luton to be relegated, but that remark got short shrift.

Having returned down south, we now faced the prospect of four successive home games and the chance to cheer ourselves up, even though the play-offs were almost out of reach. Lincoln were polished off 3-0, featuring two good strikes from Martin. A draw with promotion-chasers Grimsby saw a highly encouraging display in which Lawless' second-half strike was scant reward. Highly placed Newport also took a point from Kenilworth Road in a 2-2 draw, Gray and Jolley enhancing their reputations in front of the cameras with two well-taken goals apiece. Youngster Wall had put in some eye-catching cameo performances since his arrival, and was finally rewarded when he bagged a goal in each half to send Ebbsfleet home pointless and heading for relegation. After the game, the club announced Brill, Ainge, Rowe-Turner and Rendell were being released, and this experienced quartet would become part of a fourteen-man exodus as Still began clearing the decks for next season.

The campaign ended with the first away win in seven weeks, at Southport, a routine affair ending 3-1, Gray taking his tally for the season to twenty and Robinson notching the first of his career. It saw us end up in seventh place, a massive thirteen points short of the play-off zone. Envious eyes were cast towards Mansfield, who lifted the title, and Newport, who beat Wrexham at Wembley to win the play-off showdown.

A week after Luton's undistinguished season had crawled to a close, we long-time fans were fed news that rubbed salt into some old wounds. Politician Brian Mawhinney, former chairman of the Football League, had his autobiography published in which he devoted a number of passages to the controversial and unprecedented deduction of thirty points from Luton in 2008, which subsequently sent us skittering down the leagues into the Conference. In addition to the book's contents, Mawhinney elaborated about Luton in interviews to publicise the book. A session with the *Peterborough Evening Telegraph* was particularly revealing. Luton fans were astonished to hear Mawhinney claim he actually 'saved' Luton rather than condemned them. The *PET*'s Duncan Jackson asked him, 'Are you proud of handing a vindictive and wholly disproportionate penalty to Luton Town, condemning them to non-League football, where they remain stuck four years on?'

The reply was startling:

> Without me and the board Luton Town would not exist today. There would be no Luton Town. Someone would have had to have started a new one. It was me and the board who changed the rules to give Luton Town the possibility of salvation after 13 years of very bad leadership. We chose to exercise our discretion to save the club when literally no one else could. Am I proud of that? Yes I am.

Mawhinney was referring to rules he introduced that allowed the application of 'exceptional circumstances' to clubs that failed to achieve a Creditors Voluntary Agreement (CVA), which allowed stricken clubs back into the League, albeit with points penalties, a mechanism introduced in 2003, shortly after Mawhinney had been appointed chairman of the League, a position he held till 2010. Ten of the thirty-point penalty imposed in summer 2008 came from the FA, not the League, and Mawhinney commented on this:

> I wrote to [the FA] to express extreme displeasure that they were interfering in the internal affairs of the Football League, and that we were perfectly capable of disciplining and saving Luton without their help, but they didn't withdraw

the deduction. To this day it is a given in club and town that [Luton's] relegation, which was so hard on the club's many real fans, was solely due to the League and it's 'ringleader' that villain Mawhinney – you may substitute a harsher epithet, Luton fans did.' On that latter point, it is ironic that the song roared out with great ferocity in 2014 by Luton fans, '**** the FA, we're on our way back', doesn't even mention the League.

Perhaps Mawhinney's most astonishing postulation was this: 'As for relegation, Luton got relegated because they weren't good enough.' As we all know, the thirty-point penalty left us with twenty-six points instead of the fifty-six actually won in 2008/09, a tally that would have placed us fifteenth and not twenty-fourth. Another of his Lordship's little gems in the book was his opinion that Luton fans 'have a chip on their shoulder' over these matters. Chip? More like a giant baked potato, I'd say.

Turning attention back to the here and now, Hatters chairman Nick Owen spoke for most of us when he reflected back on the 2012/13 season and called it 'wretched' – the campaign he'd least enjoyed in fifty-five years as a fan. As he pointed out, losing at home and away to both Braintree and Dartford could only be described as inexplicable. Another mind-blowing thought was that we failed to score in three hours of action against AFC Telford, a club that broke the record for the longest run of Conference matches without a win. Seventh place in the fifth tier of English football represented our lowest finishing position ever, but in the two months since John Still's arrival there had been indications that better times could be on the horizon. When asked about the future, the new manager smiled benignly, repeated his mantra about this being a long-term project, and refused to guarantee success in 2013/14 season, our fifth in the Conference. But then he had to say that, didn't he?

5

2013/14 Season

August 2013: Here, There and Everywhere

Who would have predicted this a few years ago? Five successive summers for Luton fans with only Conference action to look forward to. The twelve weeks without competitive football can drag a little sometimes, and this time round the effect was magnified with no London Olympics, no World Cup and only a depressing series of Test defeats by the Aussies to distract us. However, this writer's summer actually flashed by in the blink of an eye due to moving house. There's nothing quite like a relocation for using up time, energy and creating stress. The thing is, having pitched up in a new neck of the woods in eastern England, I've already bumped into fellow Hatters based around here. This has strengthened my long-held theory that wherever you are in the UK (possibly wherever you are on Planet Earth), you are never more than a couple of hundred metres away from a fellow Luton supporter.

Exiles from Luton don't always speak well of their old hometown, but they do tend to fly the flag for the football team wherever they end up living. The advent of replica shirts has helped us identify each other, of course. These days many of us use Luton tops as 'casual wear' as a matter of course, perhaps forgetting we are making a bold statement by doing so. For this is not your common Arsenal or Manchester United shirt, this is the symbol of a very special underdog, a spirited little club whose loyal fan base has endured far more ups and downs than your average modern football fan. In faraway places, this shirt sparks curiosity, amusement and sometimes abuse – but when seen by fellow supporters it produces big smiles, genuine delight and a great sense of kinship. This sort of thing cannot have happened in the old days before replica shirts were widely available.

That kinship would be rekindled on Saturday 10 August when we embarked on the new season's big dipper ride with a trip to sunny Southport. Such is the nature of the sport and the mindset of the majority of its followers, optimism is always in the air at this time of year, whoever you are and whatever league in which you toil. In the wake of the Norwich FA Cup triumph seven months ago, a degree of gloom had descended on Kenilworth Road, but now there was something a little different in the air. It had been prompted by the new manager having a major clear-out, bringing in at least seven significant signings, plus a new coach, a new kit, major improvements to the training ground and healthy season ticket sales of close to 4,500. We even trounced Arsenal and Aston Villa in preseason friendlies.

Although John Still had been in his office for more than twenty weeks now, the feeling of a fresh start was only really kicking in now. Changes in playing staff were a big part of this. There were some serious mistakes during the Paul Buckle era, notably the expensive recruitment of Gillingham pair Spiller and Richards a year before. At the time they looked important and experienced captures, but neither had managed a single competitive game in the twelve months since. It emerged that both were carrying career-threatening injuries that were not brand new, and this had inevitably sparked speculation and gossip over whether this was pure bad luck or whether the problems should have been identified earlier. The fire had been fuelled by caustic exchanges on social media involving fans and the two players themselves. Maybe the full facts will never be known, but the fans' anger centred on the fact big wages were being paid for no return, and all against a backdrop of a dressing room culture where some individuals appeared more interested in a sideline of selling health supplements than winning football matches.

A successful season is usually founded upon a good start, so disappointment hung heavy in the air when we returned from Southport smarting from defeat to the only goal of the afternoon. To deepen the depression, we missed a penalty and had a man sent off. After all those summer weeks without football, this was a huge anti-climax for all, especially for the 800-plus who had made the long journey north. The day was summed up by the normally chipper voice of the manager sounding distinctly deflated in post-match interviews. Still reckoned it was a loss nobody had seen coming but admitted it was fully deserved. Five of the new signings were in the action at Haig Avenue – Luke Guttridge, Andy Parry, Shaun Whalley, Mark Cullen and Anthony Charles – but the only man to locate the onion bag was home debutant Milligan with a 25-yard first-half free-kick. There was little sparkle from Luton, Whalley fluffing a spot-kick against his former club, and to cap it all, McNulty was red carded for alleged violent conduct (later rescinded on appeal). At least we were in good company, for Premier League title-contenders Arsenal began their campaign with a shock 0-3 home defeat to unfancied Aston Villa.

It took more than an hour of the midweek home game with Salisbury to begin putting things right again, Taiwo confidently converting a penalty, followed by Guttridge nodding in a Martin free-kick. Many were surprised to see Gray on the bench, but he made a big impact after coming on, so the manager clearly knew what he was doing. Our most dangerous attacker hadn't looked up to speed preseason, according to Still, who seemed to be sending out a message here. Gray did get a starting place the following Saturday at home to Macclesfield, but it wasn't a particularly happy return as we struggled to find momentum. The visitors were at least our match, and deservedly led when former Hatter Kissock's cross was converted by Holroyd, his mishit shot creeping into the corner. Deep into stoppage time, our desperate attempts to equalise finally bore fruit when Shaw and Gray set up Guttridge to jubilantly slide the ball home. Four points from three games represented a very moderate start, and we could only hope the team would click properly into gear soon.

Forest Green Rovers had been made early season favourites for the title by the bookies, the first time in five years anyone but Luton carried this burden. They provided lively opposition down in verdant Nailsworth, and a solid, disciplined Luton display saw the contest end goalless – a reasonable return considering FGR hit eight on the opening day against Hyde. We had a few injury problems, but maybe, just maybe, things were slowly coming together. It was very early days, but it was still not nice to see Luton lingering in mid-table. Cambridge United were the early pacemakers and came to Kenilworth Road on the August Bank Holiday to provide a stern test. It was a high-tempo affair and Tyler was kept busy, although neither side showed the flair to excite a good crowd of over 7,500. Another game ended goalless, and although Guttridge was looking like an excellent signing, we seemed to be missing the guile of injured Lawless. The energetic Whalley hadn't had a great start to his career on the wings once graced by the likes of Bingham, French, Aston and Valois. He looked very direct and willing to go hell for leather every time he got the ball, but his control seemed wayward and was perhaps more reminiscent of a Perry Groves than a Chris Waddle.

Only two goals were conceded in the first five games, but the lack of success at the other end was frustrating. Cullen, Shaw and Wall were all injured and the need to bolster the strike force was becoming urgent. Still took action with an exciting signing, five days before the deadline, getting lanky centre-forward Paul Benson from Swindon on a season-long loan, a man he knew well from Dagenham days. Benson was pushing thirty-four, scored goals for the Wiltshire club under Paolo di Canio, and now seemed surplus to their requirements. He could be just the partner Gray, and maybe Cullen, had needed for a while now. There were suggestions Benson would need a week or two to get fully fit, but Still rushed him straight into the side at Kidderminster and the move proved well justified.

Benson, wearing No. 26, looked at home directing operations when we went forward, and he brought a deadlocked encounter to life in the second half when a collision with the home 'keeper after a bad back pass was deemed worthy of a penalty. Howells netted emphatically, right in front of the 821 travelling fans, and repeated the trick 10 minutes later after Gray was brought down. The 2-0 win left us still languishing down in eleventh place, but the month's batch of six league games had ended in far brighter fashion than it began. There were signs some momentum was being achieved following a very sluggish start.

September 2013: Skipper Ron Has a Quiet Word

The folks at the new BT Sport channel kindly left us alone in August, giving us time to settle into some sort to form before they swooped with their live television cameras on both our first two games of September. But then, true to form, the live television jinx struck us again. We got bogged down at home to Grimsby in a goalless draw, and followed that with a poor display and 0-2 defeat at Wrexham. A series of half-chances were created against the resolute Mariners, but we looked unconvincing in the danger area and the first half was marred by a serious-looking injury that forced off defender Alex Lacey, arguably the most promising of our younger players at the time. Versatile Parry went into defence and Stevenson came on to give an encouraging display, but nobody could conjure up a breakthrough, not even the wily Benson, who looked desperate to get off the mark with his new club. We'd gone almost 400 minutes without conceding a goal, but the shortage at the other end (just five in seven games) was prompting grumbles from the terraces.

Before the game at Wrexham, Still went public with his concerns about the moaning and groaning that seemed to have become an accepted part of life at Kenilworth Road in recent years. Money had had a bellyful of it, Buckle and Brabin suffered to a slightly lesser extent, and even the fans' favourite Harford was not immune. But Still seemed determined to knock it on the head early and rid match days of the negativity that can build quickly when things don't go favourably during a game. It was something he'd been warned about when he took the job, and something he no doubt expected would flare up now and again, given the very high expectation levels attached to this club. Now he'd seen and experienced it from the inside, he was taking steps to counter it. He was filmed in his office giving a lengthy and impassioned plea for the crowd to get behind the team at all times, especially if and when things were going badly. Still did this well, successfully negotiating the thin line between alienating fans further and bringing them on board. One of his greatest weapons was his ability to avoid sounding condescending, pompous or ill-tempered. He talked the fans' language, talked it simply and without pretence, and was persuasive. He constantly referred to how grateful the club and its players were for the huge turnouts they got every week, and commented what a fantastic weapon this would be if everyone making up those numbers was 100 per cent positive and encouraging for 90 minutes.

What Still's big PR push didn't really need was to be immediately followed by a rank display from the team. The less said about the 0-2 defeat at Wrexham the better. At least the manager was prepared to hold his hands up at the end and admit responsibility for picking the incorrect team for the job. Whalley and Cullen had come back into the starting line-up in place of Gray and the injured Lacey, but both ended up substituted in a game of zero cohesion and threat from Luton. The only welcome sight was the return at last of Lawless, a sub on the hour mark, but that was offset by fellow sub Wall being red carded for a raising a foot in the vicinity of Ashton and then appearing to stamp on him in the tangle that followed. Wall is a big man and when his massive foot goes near anybody's face, even the most generous of referees will act. Five goals scored in eight games was a dreadful return for a side with genuine promotion hopes, especially one that contains the likes of Gray, Benson, Cullen and Guttridge. As one fellow scribe said, it meant our midweek encounter with Dartford four days later had become a must-win affair.

Lawless returned to the starting line-up against the Darts for a Tuesday night game between the teams placed fourteenth and nineteenth in the Skrill Premier. The gate of 5,433, still far above anybody else's average at this level, was nevertheless a fair drop on recent Luton crowds. Lawless put in a Man of the Match display, and good work on the right by him set up Benson's first goal for the club, a simple header. He celebrated enthusiastically in the Maple Road corner of the ground, and it was a moment that seemed to settle the team and the crowd. A second goal soon followed, Howells' long run ending with Guttridge thumping the ball in from distance, helped by a deflection. Victory was assured after the interval when Smith's forward ball was flicked on by Benson and Lawless jinked around the 'keeper and fired in from a difficult angle. This was much more like it and folk were cheerful again, with the added bonus of a sixth clean sheet in nine games.

The season was only six weeks and nine games old, but with all that had gone on, it felt as if we'd already had a few months' worth of the Hatters' roller-coaster ride. And if ever a game encapsulated that point, it was the tussle at home with Lincoln City. Power shot the Imps into a first-half lead, but Luton hit back within seconds of the restart, Cullen heading us level. Tomlinson's headed goal 6 minutes later came as a shock, but Town clawed their way back level a second time when a 25-yard free-kick by Guttridge squirmed past Farman into the net. With all guns blazing, the chase for a late winner was successful when Cullen rifled the ball high into the net from close range to make it 3-2. Six goals and six points won in just five days had pointed us back in the right direction, so it was a surprise to see skipper Henry having a heated verbal exchange with a supporter near the tunnel after the final whistle.

It emerged that Henry and his colleagues had taken considerable verbal stick from this fan when leaving the field 0-1 down at half-time, and Henry was now taking the opportunity to make a point about people being too quick to criticise when encouragement might be more constructive. McNulty and O'Donnell bustled over and helped shepherd Henry away from potential trouble, but this was never fisticuffs, more a frank exchange of views. The incident would later gain considerable attention and be cited as something of a turning point in Luton's season, the moment when the message about negativity was really rammed home and began to have an effect. Interviewed afterwards, Henry would explain that he invited the fan in question to come into the ground for a chat during the week about how beneficial it would be to achieve 'togetherness' in this important season. Henry agreed most Luton fans were great, but there were a few bad apples whose constant abuse and barracking was not only out of order but actually affecting performances. Henry reckoned if this could be stamped out and everybody began pulling together 100 per cent, the team would become unstoppable in this league.

Three days later, the goals continued to flow in the clash at Woking, where Luton erased nasty memories of that 3-1 defeat on this ground on New Year's Day. More than a third of the crowd at the Kingfield Stadium were Lutonians, and the 4-0 victory went down a treat. Corner-kicks led to Cullen and Lacey netting, the former aided by a huge deflection, before Cullen powerfully headed his second from a Guttridge cross to make it 3-0 at the break. All three came at the end where the Town fans were positioned. It was no surprise when Gray was put clear to confidently make it four. It was a first-class win, the entire side looking sharp and fully motivated despite the humble surroundings. The three points saw us up to fifth, and prospects were looking brighter as those autumn leaves begin to fall from the trees.

The final Saturday of the month saw Benson return from injury to lead the attack at Hereford, Gray unluckily having to drop to the bench to make way, but Still knew the shape he wanted and was in no mood to mess around. A less pragmatic manager might have done things differently, but Still had a plan and was sticking with it. Events at Edgar Street panned out somewhat differently to those at Woking four days earlier, and a game short on goalmouth excitement would go down in the memory as a rather scrappy 0-0. It could have gone either way and was generally seen afterwards as a point gained. It was good to see the remarkable run of clean sheets maintained. Still hadn't been able to regularly field an unchanged back four, but whoever played seemed well drilled and, under Sergeant McNulty's directions, was coping well with what came their way.

October 2013: No Such Thing as a Luton 'Casual'

The post Henrygate effect became apparent at Kenilworth Road when AFC Halifax were the visitors, newly promoted, loving life in the Skrill Premier and on the same number of points (twenty) as Luton. Today, it became crystal clear that not only had recent events quietened the handful of persistent boo-boys, but the special effort the manager and captain asked for was being produced in spades. With barely 25 minutes on the clock we found ourselves, horrendously, 1-3 behind, but instead of the usual grumbling, the noise levels actually seemed to increase as home fans urged Luton back into the game. In this remarkable match, the excitement never dwindled, and by half-time we had responded to the crowd and were level again at 3-3, thanks to fine finishes from Benson and Gray. No jeers this time as they went off for their slices of orange.

Some Luton teams of recent years might have crumbled after going 1-3 down in these circumstances, but Still's ethic of 'all in this together' had clearly been embraced to yield instant results. Halifax struggled to keep us at bay in the second-half, but cracked in the 83rd minute when Wall picked up the ball on the left, took a few giant strides and hammered a monumental 25-yarder into the top corner. The ground was in raptures – a marvellous goal to win a game that would live long in the memory. It was a win achieved by 'Team Luton', just like Still and Henry had explained. As the players went into their regular post-match huddle, the manager pulled the latest of his various PR master strokes – he went and found the grumbling supporter who had confronted Henry at the Lincoln game. The new convert was invited to join the huddle and even allowed to give a little speech to the players. Still was evidently letting events speak for themselves, for not only did he get this fan to conduct the huddle, coach Hakan Hayrettin was sent out to do the post-match media duties. Significantly, HH used this opportunity to thank the crowd for their efforts no fewer than five times in one radio interview.

It had been a big day in many respects, not just for the dramatic victory, or the world-class winning goal, but for the way the supporters participated. The fans' spokesman in cyberspace, David Mosque, certainly noticed it too and pointed out,

I think Luton has a higher percentage of fans of the intense variety than other clubs. There are more Luton nuts in percentage terms than there are Arsenal nuts. You don't get so many casual Luton fans – if you are a Hatter you're in. You're along for the ride, rain or shine. It tends to be all or nothing. Once bitten fully by the Luton bug you remain bitten, whether you can still get to games or not. This is what marks us out as different. Have some of our fans been a bit moany lately? Yes. Is there a cause for that? Hell yes. Do I think Luton fans are special compared to other clubs? Yes – because of the very nature of our shared history and the numbers still coming. Do I personally think it's right to go to a match to constantly whine and shout at the players rather than give support? No. But do I think we've turned the corner. Political spin doctors can only dream of the recent events concerning Ronnie Henry and the confrontation with fan Mark. You couldn't pay for better PR. To confront him at the end of the game and then invite him to discuss his differences was inadvertent genius. For the club and the fan to link up at the training ground and for Mark to then be given the chance to apologise and to share his views and passion and the reason for his problems with the performances was a master-stroke. To go one better and for John Still to bring him on the pitch to give a post-match talk to the players after a wonderful win is pure Roy of the Rovers. You couldn't make it up.

On a high, the team headed south to face Andy Scott's Aldershot Town three days later. They were newly relegated after a spell of five seasons in the promised land of the Football League. Another first-half goalfest ensued, Gray getting things going with an early curling shot, set up by ex-Shots man Guttridge. Former Town loanee Goodman equalised from close range, but with barely 16 minutes on the clock, Parry made it 2-1 after McNulty headed on Howells' corner. Lacey and McNulty were then caught out by a long ball and Roberts levelled for a second time. Soon after a Benson penalty appeal was waved away, Moseley cracked home a fine solo goal to give the home side the lead at the break. Town's search for an equaliser was floundering until Still sent on Wall and Whalley to liven things up. Minutes later, Whalley burst into the box and was sent sprawling to win a penalty. Despite his miss from the spot at Southport, he bravely stepped up again and netted coolly for 3-3. The point took us to fourth, but Still was not entirely happy with what he called an 'unconvincing' display.

The following Saturday felt a little like the 'good old days' at the Kenny, nothing to do with struggling visitors Hyde but because the club had opened the Oak Road end of the ground to home fans for the first time in twenty-two years. For decades, this cramped and noisy little stand was the section occupied by the noisier, more laddish element of our crowd, the ones who started the songs, bounced up and down, the ones who seemed to have the most fun. I can vouch for the fact that the atmosphere in there was amazing, complete with forward and sideways surges, and of course the occasional outbreak of trouble if 'foreigners' infiltrated. By 1991, it was filled with seats and given over to away fans only. This was one of the less popular changes made at the ground during that period. The plastic pitch was torn up, what is now known as the David Preece Stand was constructed, and the away fans ban ended. The first visitors to exclusively occupy the 2,274 seats in our beloved Oak Road stand were those from Liverpool at a 0-0 draw in August 1991. Ever since that day away, fans have commented, usually disparagingly, about the unusual Oak Road entrances that go through terraced houses. The new arrangement would only be possible if visiting clubs didn't bring huge numbers of supporters, and with only thirty accompanying little Hyde, they were easily accommodated elsewhere. More than 1,200 Luton fans filed into the Oak Road end, and the atmosphere was noticeably improved with home fans now on all four sides of the pitch.

The new wave Oak Roaders get plenty of early action at their end, treated to a fine goal by Gray on 16 minutes. Hyde, winless and with just two points on the board, grabbed a shock equaliser just before half-time when McNulty horribly misdirected a header into his own net. It was a freak goal, but it was only a matter of time before the lead was regained; Gray squaring for Guttridge to slide home. Moments later, the game was won as Benson flicked on and Gray volleyed a superlative effort into the roof of the net from the corner of the area. A contender for goal of the season surely? Ashworth was red carded for man-handling Gray as he streaked through on goal. This merely delayed the inevitable hat-trick, Gray crashing home Lacey's header after a corner. After his indifferent start to the season, the lad was on fire, as they say, and bursting with confidence.

It was just as well there was plenty to enjoy against Hyde, for we now entered a six-week spell of six games, none of which were at home. The unbeaten run encouraged around 1,200 to make the trip to Tamworth, a figure that meant we outnumbered home fans at the leafy venue known as The Lamb. The home side started well in autumnal sunshine and went ahead when Courtney converted a low right-wing cross. Goals from Smith were as rare as hen's teeth, but it was he who equalised, lofting home from distance after being supplied by the lively Guttridge. A measured shot from Parry then put Luton ahead after sustained pressure just before half-time. Seconds after the restart, Benson netted a vital third with a far-post header from a deep Whalley cross. We surged 4-1 ahead when Gray outpaced the defence to square for a simple goal for Benson. Eleven goals in just over three-and-a-half games is a splendid tally, but Luton could not relax as Tamworth made attacking substitutions and gave it a real go. In the final half hour, Elford-Alliyu converted a penalty and then Courtney hooked his second into the bottom corner to make it 3-4. Luton lived dangerously in a nervy final 15 minutes in the rain, but somehow hung on. A spectacular rainbow over the motorway guided home hordes of happy Hatters.

Eight unbeaten and things were shaping up nicely in the Conference, so Still wisely shuffled his pack and rested key players for the FA Cup fourth qualifying round tie at Woking. Justham enjoyed an impressive debut in goal and Town eased through thanks to the only goal of the tie; Cullen heading home a Martin corner in the first period.

November 2013:
'Cambridge United, We're Coming for You!'

Gateshead's recent good form meant our trip north was always going to be tricky, but there was never any danger of a repeat of the 5-1 hammering they had dished out six months previously. That was then and this was now. Still was pleased his work was beginning to pay dividends and the side looked in far better shape than when he arrived. Perhaps the real heroes of the day were the 300-plus fans making this marathon journey in bad weather. Although it kicked off in sunshine, the second half saw rain lashing down and Still called conditions as bad as he's ever managed in. The pitch remained firm, as did Town's defence, and the contest ended goalless. In the circumstances, Still was spot on when he remarked that Luton had proved they were 'no soft southerners' on this grim Tyne and Wear afternoon. Perhaps the best moment of all for the fans was the news from Southport that league leaders Cambridge had lost for the first time this season. After seventeen games apiece, they were now seven points ahead of third-placed Luton. Was this the Cambridge 'blip' we'd all been waiting for?

A strong, but not entirely first-choice side tackled Welling at Park View Road in the first round proper of the FA Cup, slumping two goals behind by half-time. Benson rose to head us back into it, but the homely Kent club hung on grimly in the face of late pressure and Town went out. It was the greatest club Cup competition in the world, and the previous season's run had given us huge pleasure, but I sensed few were shedding tears over this defeat. Overhauling Richard Money's Cambridge was the real challenge this winter, and Cup distractions wouldn't be helpful.

So had we truly turned the corner under Still? Was there something about this new-look Luton that was missing during the Buckle and Brabin eras? If ever there was a single venue where these questions could be answered it was at Braintree's little Cressing Road home, or the Amlin Stadium, as they preferred it to be known these days. We'd lost on both previous visits to this ground, which constantly gave its ambitious incumbents drainage problems.

Away fans had to use an uncovered strip of terracing known as the Quag End, which is presumably a witty reference to the softness underfoot. It was as neat and tidy as they could make it, but this was a club in sore need of a new stadium, and they knew it.

Gray went on a long diagonal run, outpacing opponents, and squared the ball for Lawless, whose shot was blocked. It fell to Parry, whose effort was going wide until Benson intervened and stabbed in. The scorer made straight for a large advertising hoarding bearing the word 'Benson' and sat down beside it (to the bemusement of the Braintree fans on the other side of the wall), a bizarre but original celebration. It was 2-0 when a corner was whipped over by Lawless and a scramble ensued, Parry forcing the ball over the line in front of the massed ranks from Luton. Cue major celebrations, which were marred only slightly when referee Amey made a big show of calling Parry over and booking him, presumably for over-celebrating with the crowd. It seemed a puzzling and petty decision. From our point of view, the sheer enthusiasm and all-inclusiveness of the goal celebrations showed how together this side was.

Braintree pulled a goal back quickly, Holman's shot looping crazily off a defender's foot to fly out of Tyler's reach. There were 23 minutes still to go, and with McNulty and Benson carrying injuries and forced off the field, suddenly it was backs-to-the-wall stuff. Parry went to centre-half and played a major part in keeping the scores level. In the dying seconds, he made a brilliant last-ditch clearance to prevent an undeserved equaliser. The final whistle went immediately, and Tyler and others rushed to hug Parry for a tackle that was worth two league points. It had been a scruffy, blood-and-guts victory on a horrendous pitch, but it gave enormous satisfaction. It wasn't pretty Luton passing football, but this was what you had to do to win this league. Still was delighted and called it one of the best all-round performances of the season. Suddenly the cold, damp Essex night didn't seem so forbidding, especially when we heard Kidderminster had only drawn, allowing us to leapfrog into second place. Cambridge remained seven points clear, but Luton fans were now singing with great conviction a new refrain: 'Cambridge United, we're coming for you...'

The batch of half-a-dozen successive away games ended with a trip to Chester, where traffic problems delayed Luton's team bus and the kick-off had to be pushed back. All this messing around didn't affect Gray, who turned and rifled Luton ahead early on, but Seddon was able to hit back with a long-range equaliser. Chester were in the bottom four but conjured up their best display of the season, and a draw seemed to satisfy both sides.

Welling also put up a spirited display when they came to Bedfordshire, and the in-form Gray's confident finishing was the main factor separating the sides. This was not the Hatters' most cohesive display, but Gray got things moving in the right direction, burying a fine shot after a deft Benson flick. When Henry pulled down Healy soon after the interval, Tyler saved Lafayette's penalty, but the cheers were stifled as the rebound was rifled home by Dyer from a narrow angle. This put a spring into Welling's step and the spoils could have gone either way until a fine move involving Guttridge and Lawless 11 minutes from time was finished off by Gray's ninth of the season from just fourteen starts. Wings' defender Franks saw red near the end after pulling down Benson and showing dissent.

Three days later, with the prospect of a low midweek turnout of fans representing Southport (sixteen was the subsequent total), Luton opened the Oak Road end to home fans again, for only the second time since top-flight days. They added to this fan-friendly gesture by publicly backing a campaign by the Football Supporters' Federation (FSF) to bring safe standing back to football grounds. Kenilworth Road had been all-seated since the summer of 1994, but I suspect many fans welcomed the return of a standing area as long as safety was not compromised. McNulty was the unlikely scorer who got Luton's show on the road, volleying a big dipper from at least 25 yards after Southport only half-cleared a free-kick. It was one of those 1-in-1,000 strikes and sent the ground into a frenzy. If the goal was spectacular, the celebration was certainly not, the big man simply strolling back to his defensive post with barely a smile until his progress was halted by nine teammates jumping on him. Perhaps he was simply stunned. We then had to wait deep into the second half for Smith for to knock in the second, followed by Gray lashing home to make it a comfortable 3-0. Benson and Guttridge both hit the woodwork, so the Sandgrounders got off lightly. With Cambridge not in action that evening, the gap at the top is reduced to four points. 'Cambridge United, we're coming for you…' rang out loud and clear again.

With injury worries over Charles, Lacey, Parry and McNulty, Still filled his boots shortly before the November loan window closed, taking three youngsters on loan: Joe Davis from Port Vale, Alfie Mawson from Brentford and Pelly Ruddock from West Ham. To balance the books, goalkeeper Brill left permanently for Inverness CT, and O'Donnell and Stevenson were sent out on loan. Davis and Ruddock stepped straight into a very youthful side to take on Staines in the FA Trophy first round, and a debut was also given to David Viana, a precocious midfield talent of dual French and Portuguese nationality. The tie ended goalless at Wheatsheaf Park.

December 2013: Massacre of the Midlanders

This was a big month. The one when we hit the halfway point in the league programme, and the one where we started dreaming of going into the new year top of the table. Luton dropped just two points in five games during November, whereas Cambridge let four slip from four, suggesting we were now the form side to watch. At various points during the autumn we were ten points behind them, but December commenced with that gap reduced to just four. Where we stood at the end of April was what really mattered of course, but to arrive at New Year's Eve on top would be a huge boost, having spent the past four years hovering just below that pinnacle.

Top-six outfit Alfreton welcomed us to the Impact Arena for the month's first Conference action, on paper a very testing encounter on a sloping pitch. But those who feared this was a 'banana skin' impeding our progress to the top needn't have fretted. Featuring a sparkling performance from Guttridge, involved in everything, Luton put on a powerful display that had Still purring and his opposite number Nicky Law in a state of high angst. Between the 10th and 18th minute we knocked home no fewer than four goals, all beautifully created and executed. Alfreton were torn to shreds and Law's response was to immediately bring on a defensive substitute to try and limit the already fatal damage.

Strangely enough, given the deluge about to hit, Alfreton had started quite brightly. Then at 3.10 p.m., the massacre commenced: cue a 30-yard peach of a pass by Guttridge, sending Gray clear to whip the ball past the advancing 'keeper Atkins. Three minutes later, another astute Guttridge pass sent Benson into space to expertly clip over the goalkeeper. Alfreton were on the canvas and Luton rampant. The third goal followed just a minute later and was a real classic. Starting at the back, Town zig-zagged swiftly down the left in a pacy move involving nine first-time passes, the last of which was knocked over the line by a jubilant Gray. *In dulce jubilo!* Arsenal and Barcelona eat your hearts out. And still the fun wasn't over. Gray then returned the favour by setting up Guttridge, who slid the ball into the net from a very tight angle to make it 0-4 with still only 18 minutes having passed.

The travelling support – more than half the 1,270 gate – were in raptures, and radio and internet listeners across the globe thrashing around in delight too. Gray must have thought Christmas had come three weeks early, for the home defence held a shaky and suicidally high line and were unable to do anything about his lightning pace. Benson and Guttridge had the experience and know-how to exploit this situation, and such was their efficacy that far better sides than Alfreton would have surely struggled against us that day. Law's emergency substitution on 21 minutes helped stem the tide and there was no further scoring until the second period, when Lawless was put through by Gray and beat Atkins neatly. At 0-5 it equalled our best away win in any league match. With Cambridge involved in FA Cup action, this left us a single point behind them, albeit having played two more games.

There was evidently real belief on the field these days, and it was spreading to the terraces too. Law had little option but to be magnanimous when the reporters pressed him for a reaction to the carnage: 'You have to hold your hands up – they're a much better team than we are. They're the best that we've seen this year and the best we've come up against by a long, long way.' Still, meanwhile, struggled to conceal a grin of satisfaction as he suggested Luton's combination play had been well above Conference level, and he repeated his new mantra about everybody on and off the pitch chipping in: – 'the stronger the team, the stronger the team'. MD Gary Sweet spoke glowingly of the style and swagger shown at Alfreton, and of the breathtaking impact Still and his sidemen had had in creating this. Still had by now signed a contract extension to 2015, which contained a stipulation that, for each promotion won, an additional year would be added.

It seemed almost a shame that while on this red-hot streak two matches should intervene in the FA Trophy, but Still called up younger fringe players, and Staines were beaten in the first round replay 2-1. The 'reserves' looked sharp and confident in beating a more experienced Wrexham side 2-0 in round two at Kenilworth Road. The serious business resumed on the last Saturday before Christmas when Gateshead came to town, just short of 7,000 turning out on a day when traditionally crowds normally dip – even more noteworthy as there was heavy rain and only twenty-three away fans in the ground.

Benson opened the scoring in a fine match between two in-form sides, heading home after a neat move down the left. Persistence by Lawless saw him wrestle possession in Gateshead's box to ram home the second. The positive attitude was underlined by Gray, who grabbed the ball 30 yards out and, with minimum fuss, strode forward to lash home a beauty before defenders could think about closing him down. In the second half, the fourth was another tremendous team goal, a move started by McNulty and Henry deep in their own half, up the flank to Gray, who rode a tackle and sprinted forward to slip it inside to Benson, who manoeuvred a shooting position, the 'keeper parrying his effort to where Lawless arrived to net with a first-time shot. An hour had gone and we were 4-0 up against a decent team – no wonder the ground was rocking like rarely before in the Conference era. We fans were greedy and demanded more goals, but inevitably the pace slackened for a spell and the visitors stole in twice late on to make it 4-2 and blot our defensive copybook. But such was the brilliance of the first 75 minutes that this failed to sour the mood, and there was the added bonus of hearing Cambridge had slipped to a second defeat of the season, at Hereford.

Luton's allocation of 1,700 tickets for a Boxing Day excursion to Barnet – or Camrose Avenue in Edgware to be precise – sold out well in advance. Under their much-decorated head coach Edgar Davids, the Bees had forced their way into play-off contention. Unlike most teams playing Boxing Day, Barnet were told not to come in for training on Christmas Day by Davids, but any hopes they might have overindulged were forgotten when Villa went close with a fierce shot early on. Luton soon found a rhythm, and after loanee Davis missed an open goal, Gray set up Benson to expertly knock home from close range. Minutes later, Lawless picked the ball up near the halfway line and raced down the left before cutting in and curling a fine drive past 'keeper Stack into the corner – it was 0-2 and another contender for goal of the season chalked up.

The away sections were bouncing with delight and anticipating another goal feast until the mood changed dramatically minutes later. It happened when Barnet striker Nurse hurtled into a crazy late challenge on Smith; the resounding crack and Smith's instant collapse meant there was little doubt his leg had been broken. There was mayhem both on and off the pitch. The incident happened close to the dugouts and the Luton manager was seen wandering around in agitation and shock, while his opposite number was equally upset, admitting later it 'turned my stomach'. Smith received extensive treatment and was stretchered off, but to everybody's amazement, referee Whitton only admonished Nurse with a yellow card. The pandemonium near the dugout continued, and after consulting his assistant and the fourth official, suddenly the referee brandished a red card at the subdued Nurse. As he trudged off, the forward was left in no doubt as to what all 1,700 away fans thought of his 'tackle', but he got words of sympathy from former Dagenham colleague Benson, who clearly believed Nurse had not intended serious injury to Smith.

Rarely had the atmosphere at a game changed so quickly. Luton battled on but had lost the momentum of earlier, and even having an extra man failed to help them put the game out of Barnet's reach. Twenty minutes from time, Hyde glanced a header past Tyler and we had to endure a nerve-wracking finish as the Bees strove for an unlikely draw. The final whistle signalled enormous roars of relief at the away end and the seventh successive league victory was in the bag. In the aftermath, Edgar Davids seemed as upset as anyone by what had happened to Smith and praised Still and Luton's players for maintaining discipline and acting professionally. Still said it affected him badly, more than he would have expected, and admitted he'd never had such a nasty episode occur so close to him in all his years in football: 'I knew it was a break because I heard it, the staff heard it and the players heard it.' This writer was probably 40 yards away, in the middle of the noisy Luton contingent, and also clearly heard it. We were told that perpetrator Jon Nurse, a thirty-two-year-old Barbados international, had never been an overly-aggressive type and had apologised profusely to all parties. Victim Smith had been very effective in midfield lately and would be sorely missed, but was known to be a very fit and dedicated trainer who would battle hard to get back.

The episode was merely the latest in the weird and not-so-wonderful tenure of ex-Dutch international Davids as Barnet player/head coach. Having been appointed just over a year earlier, Davids had had problems with his own disciplinary record, being booked or sent off in all of the first eight Bees games he played. He was praised for rescuing thirty-six stranded Barnet fans from the side of a motorway and buying them coffee on one away trip, and then made more headlines by allocating himself the No. 1 shirt traditionally worn only by goalkeepers. Recently, he provoked more controversy, announcing he wouldn't attend any away games that required an overnight stay. He dropped himself for the Luton match, but two days later played at Salisbury and picked up another red card, claiming afterwards he was being unfairly treated by officials and was considering quitting. Three weeks later he would do just that.

There were some tired Luton bodies after the Battle of Barnet, but no time to relax, for two days later action resumed at Kenilworth Road. Play-off contenders Kidderminster were the opposition for the first home game of the second half of the campaign. The manager said he was not paying any attention to Cambridge, but we fans begged to differ; we had noticed that if Luton extended their run of home wins that day and Cambridge failed to get all three points at Nuneaton, we would knock them off top spot. They'd been in pole position since mid-August (apart from nine days), while Luton had not occupied first place for sixteen months. So yes, this was a big deal.

Robinson for Smith was the only team change, although the manager himself was missing from the ground for medical reasons, hopefully only a minor problem. The game sprang into life shortly before the half-hour mark when Benson and Guttridge combined neatly to set up Robinson for a shot on goal that was parried to Guttridge to tap home. The change of ends heralded a second-half onslaught towards the Oak Road end, yielding no fewer than five more Town goals. Still was presumably listening via radio at home and wishing he'd contravened doctor's orders. A diagonal cross from Howells on the left was headed firmly home by Benson for the second. Gray then flicked through for Benson to chase into the box, where he was impeded by Dunkley; the referee gave a penalty but, unsure whether to show red or yellow, consulted his assistant and then waved a red at Gowling. Right decision, wrong man – oh, how we laughed. After a second consultation with his assistant, they picked out the correct offender. To be fair, both Dunkley and Gowling were tall and well-built fellows, but Gowling had a big afro and Dunkley's hair was cropped short. When the almighty fuss died down, Howells netted the penalty. Something similar would happen later in the season at Premier League level, referee Marriner dismissing Arsenal's Gibbs when Oxlade-Chamberlain had clearly been the guilty party.

Luton were on a roll again by now, and Gray chipped into the box for Benson to head across goal for Howells to convert an easy fourth. Town were in cruise control and a free-kick near the byeline was lofted over by Guttridge for Griffiths, possibly the shortest man on the field, to rise majestically at the near post to head his first Luton goal. It might have been modesty, or perhaps he was playing it cool, but Griffiths reacted calmly and Guttridge had to dash over and give him lessons in how to celebrate. Prior to goal number six, the 'olés' rang out as passes went smoothly from man to man, and a deflated Kiddy could not respond – I counted at least seven passes as Town flowed from their own box to the other end before Guttridge at the end of the production line to side-footed home a measured shot. It was the goal of the game and yet another candidate for best of season. I'd not seen anything like this since the golden days of ball players Hill, Moss and Preece. Check out the Youtube celebrations by Guttridge (he wiped his brow!) and the commentary by Simon Pitts ('Oh, my Lord!') if you don't believe this was something really special.

A sensational afternoon's entertainment was over, but the icing on the cake – you guessed it – was news that Cambridge had only drawn at Nuneaton, and Luton had gone top of the table at last. Hallelujah! The run of six straight victories through December also saw Still win Skrill's Manager of the Month award and striker Benson (four goals and several assists) named Player of the Month. A remarkable end to a remarkable year.

January 2014: Plucking Points from Puddles

The experts told us this mild winter had seen far more sunshine than average, but also more rain than usual. We were apparently heading for the wettest winter on record, and the weather gods in charge of Bedfordshire certainly had a good laugh when Barnet were visitors on New Year's Day. The game was live on the BT Sport channel, hence a midday kick-off, meaning there was extra pressure to get it on, even though the soggy pitch and dodgy forecast suggested trouble ahead. After two inspections, the contest got the green light, despite the managers suggesting it wasn't really playable. Right from the start, it was clear the ball was not running or bouncing properly on the drenched surface. With 7,543 inside the ground and a big live television audience, it would have needed a very brave referee to do a U-turn and call a halt once things got underway. From kick-off, the best policy seemed to be to hoof the ball high and chase after it, rather than try a short passing game. Luton had the lightning pace of Gray to pursue these forward balls, and it paid off within 2 minutes. Guttridge's flick-on arrived at the feet of Gray, who sped clear of three defenders and slammed past 'keeper Stack.

Midway through the half. Stack hobbled off injured and sub Jupp took over, soon to be beaten as Howells' cross allowed Benson to bury the ball from close range. The conditions were slowly worsening, but there was no way Luton wanted this abandoned now. Both sides splashed away gamely, but there was the constant worry of fatigue and injury resulting from all this; it was Luton's fourth big game in twelve days and there was another coming up shortly. But at least we were getting points on the board while Cambridge were idle and worrying about a backlog. There were plenty of comedy moments to enjoy, including Barnet's Marsh-Brown slipping and toppling over just when he was within sight of goal. At one point it got so bad the referee called the skippers together for a chat, but the animated figure of Henry apparently found the right words to convince him to see out the final 30 minutes. Guttridge brought a brilliant save out of Jupp, then 20 minutes from time Hyde converted a right-wing cross for 2-1, to set up a nervy ending in the quagmire. We survived a reasonable shout for a penalty when the ball struck an arm, before proceedings were brought to a halt amid huge roars of delight and relief. Cambridge's game at the regularly flooded Braintree ground had inevitably been cancelled, meaning we went four points clear at the top, having played two games more.

It was clear the current Luton squad were a fit and well-conditioned bunch, for despite the recent hectic spell and difficult pitches Still was able to select the same eleven to travel to Lincoln for another lunchtime kick-off just three days later. Our bid to extend the run of wins to eight in a row faltered in a goalless draw, but this was not an outcome to be scoffed at. Both sides went close to a winner, with Luton the more likely scorers near the finish. The work rate and spirit has been tremendous lately, and was helped in no small part by the noisy away support. Sincil Bank is the sort of place we used to hate visiting, but things had changed and we were starting to have the look of champions about us. Not too many folk were actually voicing that opinion yet, which was probably because nobody wanted to tempt fate. We'd had false dawns before, and there were still many miles to travel.

A three-week period arrived without a Conference game, but it didn't help Cambridge sort out their backlog, for they were drawn to face Luton in the FA Trophy third round, a game that then needed a replay. As the Us had a smaller squad, they fielded a near full-strength side for the Cup ties, whereas Luton put out what was effectively a second string. A 2-2 draw at the Abbey Stadium was followed by a 1-0 win for Cambridge in the replay. Luton spirits survived this minor hiccup undampened – intrusive Cup runs had helped mess up our league hopes the previous season and nobody wanted that again.

A couple of games fell victim to the weather, but Nuneaton's visit went ahead at Kenilworth Road, albeit with the prospect of stormy weather moving in. A rather forgettable opening half was followed by a tremendous second from Luton, the main feature being a 27-minute hat-trick from Gray and a dramatic hailstorm that had the players running for cover. The breakthrough goal was typical Gray, picking up a flick from Benson, brushing off challengers and hammering a shot fiercely under the 'keeper. Number two saw him tuck home a low driven cross from Griffiths, moments after a frantic scramble in the muddy goalmouth. The hat-trick goal was a nonchalant strike with the outside of his right boot after being put clear by a looping header from McNulty.

Gray now had seventeen goals from just twenty-two starts and had the Golden Boot award in his sights. He didn't look quite so cool when the storm hit, though; club photographer Gareth Owen captured the moment, the hat-trick hero looking horrified and covering his head with his hands as an incredible stinging downpour lashed him. The players and officials sprinted for shelter, but fortunately we were soon able to resume and the hat-trick and the 3-0 win didn't have to be scrubbed from the record books. A club record twenty league games without defeat had now been created and things were looking good for the run-in. Towards the end of January, Cambridge were beaten by Grimsby and held 3-3 by Dartford, the net result being a three-point lead at the top for Luton, both teams having now completed twenty-eight games.

'Strengthen the squad while you are playing well' is an old football adage, and Still used the January transfer window to do just that. He captured former loanee Ruddock from West Ham on a permanent basis, plus defender Fraser Franks from Welling, as well as taking Kane Ferdinand (Peterborough), Ryan Inniss (Crystal Palace), Cameron McGeehan (Norwich) and Jernade Meade (Swansea) all on loan. Leaving the building were loanees Davis and Mawson, returning to their normal employers; Rendell joined Woking, while Wall, O'Donnell, Stevenson, Whalley and Taiwo were all loaned out. The paperwork for that little lot must have been mountainous. Football admin was never like this in the days of Syd Owen and Wally Shanks.

February 2014: The Juggernaut Gathers Speed

We were told a misbehaving jet stream was to blame for parts of southern England spending weeks under water, which in turn contributed to decimation of the football programme. Two more Luton games were called off, leading to seventeen days without Conference action. This was not good news now that we'd hit top form, but the problems being encountered by chief rivals Cambridge were far more significant. Richard Money's men had found themselves on a nightmare run of five league games without a win. During the same period, they played three FA Trophy ties but didn't lose any of them. Money went ballistic over this, apparently believing his players were allowing cup matters to bring about a surrendering of the league title to Luton.

Inevitably, much cruel banter was being targeted towards Money from the Luton direction as the wheels started to come off the CUFC challenge. He was lampooned for comments in which he described Luton as a 'runaway train', a 'juggernaut', and 'that team from down the road'. Luton fans had great fun with all this, dreaming up plenty of suggestions over what sort of vehicle Cambridge might currently resemble. And there was certainly no feeling of surprise in the Luton camp when it was reported Money had upset Cambridge fans by accusing them of being too quiet at home games. 'I wanted to ask them, are you not entertained?' he'd moaned, although he later conceded these had been the words of 'a grumpy old fool'. What was far more surprising was an outburst he made concerning Luton; asked about the Hatters' unbeaten run, he said it was nothing special because Luton paid League One wages and played in front of 6,500 every week. This was an unexpected reaction from a manager who'd failed to exploit those very assets when he was in charge himself. On the topic of wages, it was also quietly pointed out that Cambridge had recently beaten Luton to the signature of Michael Spillane by offering higher wages. The local press loved all this and tried for a reaction from John Still, but the Luton boss refused to get involved and wouldn't talk about Cambridge at all. A wise move.

Thanks to sterling work by fork-wielding volunteers, Macclesfield's pitch just about passed muster for a Tuesday night game at Moss Rose. More than 400 Luton fans and club officials had driven through snow in the Peak District fearing the worst, but the contest survived. Within9 minutes, the prolific Gray had put us ahead, Ruddock playing a key role in a slick move that ended with Gray chipping over the flailing Taylor, possibly a cross not a shot, and it ended up in the net. The home side, arguably the toughest opponents so far this season, hit back strongly and their pressure paid off when a 20-yarder by Andrew snaked past Tyler. Fighting hard to weather the Macc onslaught, Town won a throw and Griffiths hurled it into the danger area, where Gray swivelled to hook the ball past a shocked 'keeper. Tyler had a brilliant match as Town repelled attack after attack, and came away with three of the hardest-earned points in many a month. This really was promotion style, and the news that Cambridge had lost at home on the same night was the icing on the cake. It meant Luton went six points clear at the top, both challengers having seventeen games apiece remaining.

After the true grit shown at Macclesfield, a different type of challenge followed when Martin Foyle's inconsistent but potentially dangerous Hereford came to Kenilworth Road. The rumour mill suggested Still planned to defy his doctor's advice by attending the game, having missed out on a 6-0 win last time he listened to his medics. As we would see, he made a good call and the performance his team subsequently gave must have helped his healing processes! The manager's health issues were, of course, a private matter, but inevitably discussion was prompted among fans over what might have been wrong; one wag suggested his recent hospital visit had been to have a halo fitted, while another reckoned he went in to have his 'controllables controlled'.

All in all, the build-up to the Hereford game had been quite a week at Kenilworth Road. Smith was seen strolling around the place without the aid of crutches, barely seven weeks since his leg had been broken. There was also much fuss over special plastic rain covers being shipped in from Scotland to protect the pitch from continuing bad weather. And there was drama on the eve of Hereford's visit when superfan John Pyper reported seeing the new covers flapping around uselessly after being dislodged in gale force winds – his emergency call to the stadium manager apparently saved the day. The battered pitch was surrounded by sandbags as we all took our seats next day, and among the big crowd were members of the Luton Town Supporters Club of Scandinavia, complete with Viking fancy dress and jovial Nordic singing voices.

The irrepressible Gray got the show on the road, poaching the first goal when McGeehans's shot was only half saved on 12 minutes. Hereford battled hard to stem the tide and held out until minutes after the restart, McGeehan rising high to a corner, his header touched in by Benson. As he crashed to the ground, McGeehan picked up an unusual injury, described later as a hyper-extended elbow. A very painful thing, but he's a cheerful chappie and it failed to spoil his week, which also included an Irish under-21 call-up and an extension of his loan from Norwich. His goal opened the floodgates. Seven minutes later, Ruddock took a return pass and was up-ended for a clear penalty, which Howells confidently struck home. It was soon 4-0 when a wonderfully incisive move involving four players and one-touch passing ended with Ruddock lashing the ball high into the net – the sort of team goal that had become a trademark lately.

Poor Hereford hardly knew what had hit them. The 7,111 crowd was in raptures, screaming for more of the same, and they duly got it. The fifth goal arrived when Benson tracked back to dispossess an opponent, found Guttridge, whose chip forward set Gray away to net with precision. Lawless' run down the left then set up Gray to complete a hat-trick and make it twenty-two for the season and fifty in his relatively short Luton career so far. Hereford just wanted the misery to be over, but there was one final twist of the knife to come. Robinson's free-kick saved, the ball flew high in the air only to end in the back of the net courtesy of the inrushing Lawless and Shaw. Both initially claimed the goal, but the verdict eventually favoured the former. This 7-0 drubbing matched Hereford's worst ever, and embarrassed club officials offered to compensate the 156 travelling fans with a free buffet meal later on. Luton's unbeaten run now stood at twenty-two Conference games, which helped ensure demand for tickets for the forthcoming trip to Cambridge would be hotter than ever. Those of us not living close to the LTFC ticket office began phoning early in the morning to reserve one, unaware we were fighting a losing battle against a huge queue of personal callers outside the ground. The allocation of tickets quickly sold out, but after pressing 'redial' repeatedly for nearly seven hours I finally got through and was put on a reserve list in case Cambridge released any extra tickets. At this stage it was looking like yours truly, and many other season ticket holders, would have to miss out on the big game; our angst led to much grumbling on the social media sites. However, the Cambridge public didn't show the same enthusiasm for the game as at the Luton end, meaning more tickets did indeed become available to us, and most people were catered for. Luton's beleaguered ticket office staff and their distribution policies deservedly ended up with more bouquets than brickbats on this occasion.

The long queue for tickets outside Luton's ground had been a real blast from the past. Those of us stuck on phones many miles away, who missed this nostalgic sight, got the skinny from Kevin Crowe in his *Left Midfield* blog update:

The queue from the Kenilworth Road ticket office stretches back to the scruffy corner of Beech Path. No one's interested in work today. For these men, women, boys and girls are the cagouled collateral of a renaissance ... the rosy-cheeked queue for Cambridge away tickets said as much about our season as Andre Gray's thumping hat-tricks or Paul Benson's swooping diving header at Nuneaton; the buzz from the Portakabin counters of the ticket office, an equally valid onomatopoeia. Because as I write this we sit eleven points clear. ELEVEN. Savour this feeling boys and girls. This is what makes that empty main stand and all that stick off your mates at school worthwhile ... after five years, like 7,000 battle-scarred Shane MacGowans crooning *Dirty Old Town* through a new set of brilliant white false teeth, we smell the spring on the smoky wind. And wouldn't it be great to get back into the sunshine.

The wind-battered Liberty Way, home of Nuneaton Town, was our next port of call, and there was more big fun in store. A remarkable tally of 1,991 Luton fans – more than many Championship sides take to away games – helped make it a ground record of 3,480 for the Midlanders. Benson put us in front, skipping around the 'keeper after scuffing his first attempt. For the second week running, there was a second-half goal avalanche, this time kicked off when Benson's diving header at the far post was touched over the line by Gray. A neat passing move was then finished by Guttridge, powering home from the edge of the box. Nine minutes from time came the inevitable fourth, a deft diving header by Benson from a Howells cross.

At this point, many home fans began heading for the exits, fed up with the humiliation being dished out. Instead of the usual 'cheerio, cheerio' from the celebrating Luton contingent, somebody came up with a new one: 'Is there a fire drill? Is there a fire drill?' Howells rose to make it 5-0, heading in sub Shaw's centre. The fans were determined to enjoy this rich vein of form while it lasted, and some of the slick passing was a treat to behold, contradicting the naysayers who had warned that under John Still we would suffer unattractive, route one football. With Cambridge eleven points adrift and getting closer to Wembley in the FA Trophy, it was tempting to think the league was now all over bar the shouting, but with fifteen games left, we were hearing nothing of the sort from Kenilworth Road, even though management were at least allowing themselves to occasionally use the 'P' word (promotion) in conversation.

A bumper crowd gathered under the lights on the final Tuesday in February, demanding more goals from Europe's most in-form professional club. Their wish was Luton's command. Wrexham, currently managerless and having a below-par season, were taken to the cleaners to the tune of four goals in the first period. There was less than 3 minutes on the clock when Benson and Howells nimbly did the spadework on the left and Guttridge continued his dazzling form to tuck the ball superbly into the bottom corner. Cue the trademark Guttridge celebration, which involved greeting the Maple Road corner of the ground with a sort of airborne version of Usain Bolt's 'lightning bolt' gesture. Barely had the cheers died down that the second goal arrived, Ashton getting in a tangle when faced by Gray, who rammed the ball home. Guttridge's turn next, and he made it 3-0 on 17 minutes, taking a short pass from Benson to finish accurately for the twelfth time this season. Not bad for a midfielder released by lowly Northampton.

The first-half masterclass ended with a fourth goal as Gray's hard work was completed by a Henry cross tucked in by the lurking Benson. A fine

move on the stroke of half-time narrowly failed to yield a fifth, and the
happy fans gave a standing ovation as the teams trooped off. Wrexham
tightened up at the back after the break, but let in one more soon after
veteran Benson was given a well-earned rest. His replacement, Shaw, set up
Howells, who was upended but picked himself up to net the penalty. The
spot-kick had been offered to Guttridge, on a hat-trick, but like a true pro
he left it to the regular taker. Another great night and a step nearer the title,
helped by news from the paddy fields of Essex that Braintree had beaten
Cambridge, leaving the latter fourteen points behind Luton with one game
in hand. With good reason, Luton fans were now crowing about the fat
lady preparing herself to sing.

It was no coincidence Luton found themselves in this healthy position,
having avoided serious fixture congestion. Below us, the recent heavy rain,
coupled with other teams' cup commitments, had left the table looking
very unbalanced. In mid-February Braintree had been faced with fitting
twenty-one of their forty-six fixtures into a nine-week period – an average
of one game every three days. Grimsby and Cambridge faced the prospect of
a game every Saturday and Tuesday till the end of the season. At one point,
Grimsby had seven games in hand on a team directly below them (Halifax)
and six on a team above (Nuneaton). But in the face of criticism over all
this, the Conference board came out fighting, saying they were tied by the
date given to them for the Wembley play-off final, and the fact FA Trophy
ties had to be played on Saturdays instead of midweek. Amid this chaos at
the end of February, Cambridge remained the only realistic challenger to
Luton's position as champions-elect. But it wasn't a very evenly matched two-
horse race – Cambridge hadn't won in five league games while the Luton
'juggernaut' was unbeaten in twenty-four, winning twelve of its last thirteen
league games and netting a phenomenal seventeen goals in the last three.

After years seeing end-of-season failure, Luton fans were currently in
dreamland. But poor Richard Money's descent into meltdown continued,
and he was by now ranting that even the play-offs were not a guaranteed
prospect for his side, let alone a title challenge. A clip of him being
interviewed after the Braintree defeat by BBC Cambridgeshire made painful
listening; he was actually shouting as he lashed out at the people from his
club who talked of the play-offs. 'We are a mile away from the play-offs,
we still need twenty-four points to reach the play-offs. We've got to get our
heads out of our backsides and start working. Listen to my words everybody
– teams can drift away.'

John Still was far too professional and cagey to start boasting about our
title chances, but at the end of the month his opposite number at Alfreton,
Nicky Law, did it for him: 'Luton are going to win this league by a long way.
John has come in and changed a lot of people's attitudes towards Luton,

they are getting respect and earning respect in the right way,' said Law. A 100 per cent record during February won Still the Manager of the Month title and Gray's seven February goals won him the Conference player award. It had been exactly a year since we welcomed Still into our midst, and he had produced results beyond most people's expectations.

He reflected on his first twelve months:

> The year has gone as well as I hoped it could have done. I didn't know how long it would take to get to where we are, but I always believed we could get here. I can remember sitting here earlier in the season writing up my programme notes, saying that opposition coming here would want to keep it quiet for 20 minutes so our crowd goes the other way. It was something I knew, somewhere along the line, we would have to address. That was part of the challenge.

A year on from watching Luton succumb 2-0 at Braintree (when he allegedly turned to assistant Terry Harris and told him to call Dagenham and say they were coming back), Still could surely now begin enjoying the fruits of one of his greatest managerial feats. He said,

> I think we've reinvented this football club. That's all of us – players, supporters and staff – who have all worked to try and get the team ethic. The thing that I was fully aware of when I came here was how many people felt that Luton weren't treated properly. To right a wrong for all those people, to give them something that they felt was taken away, I would look upon that as something special.

Everybody acknowledged Still was the main architect of the current success, but a few superstitious types believed that recognition was also due to the supporter known as Lewsey Bob. This stalwart figure had been going to great lengths lately to ensure he wore his infamous lucky pants on matchdays, and his success in locating the correct pants each time seemed to have coincided with the club's unbeaten run. We were all left hoping the garment in question survived to the end of the season at least.

Luton's lofty position was making all and sundry sit up and take notice. Perhaps some of them had even forgotten we were down here. *The Guardian* sent a reporter to the Wrexham game and he interviewed receptionist Lita Nunn, who joined the club nearly thirty years ago. She told him the club had had 'a family feeling' back in the 1980s, and that vibe was returning. Wrexham's caretaker-manager Billy Barr, a man who knew his way around the lower leagues, chipped in, 'Luton are the best team I've seen in the Conference for many, many years.' The reporter concluded his findings with the verdict this was definitely not another of those false dawns: 'Luton are not promoted yet. Not officially. But it is only a matter of time. Forget tonight's cold: the fans can feel something else in their bones. The tingle of their club emerging from the woes and blows of recent years.'

March 2014: The Fat Lady Clears Her Throat

Alfreton, battling for a play-off place, came to Kenilworth Road on the first day of the month and worked hard to frustrate free-scoring Town. Their game plan started to fall apart when Guttridge shot home at the second attempt around the half-hour mark, celebrating by pointing to an imaginary watch on his wrist. Maybe he had a Golden Goal ticket with 30 minutes on it? After the interval, good work by Griffiths set up a tap-in for Gray and it was soon 3-0 after a real comedy goal, the 'keeper drop-kicking the ball against the back of a colleague, which allowed Howells to cross for Benson to score comfortably. Twenty goals scored and none conceded in the last four games was a statistic to savour, as was the fourteen-point lead at the top.

A rather scruffy 0-0 in the sun at Salisbury City a week later saw Town looking a little tired without the injured and influential Guttridge, and with Franks and Gray having played for England 'C' in Jordan a few days earlier. After negotiating some very precarious concrete steps to get to the pitch, the players had to cope with a surface that cut up and didn't favour passing football – 'a bit like playground football', said Still. Just a few miles away, Cambridge lost a five-goal thriller at Forest Green, allowing us to move fifteen points clear at the top, having played one game more. That gap was a huge psychological advantage to be carrying into the following Tuesday's showdown at Cambridge.

Because of Luton's huge lead, the contest at the Abbey Stadium was no longer the crunch affair it might have been; failing to win would all but end Cambridge's dwindling hopes of the title. The ground hummed to the tune of a 6,050 crowd, Luton selling out their allocation and roared on by a travelling army of 2,286. Richard Money's programme notes were unexpectedly magnanimous and will have gone some way to easing the bad feeling between him and the Luton fans. He wrote about the highlights of his forty-two-year career and called his stint as a Luton player the most memorable of all, admitting that failing to take Luton back into the Football League remained one of his biggest regrets.

But few had the time or inclination to read programme notes due to the gut-wrenching tension surrounding this game. It was an absorbing, deadlocked affair for more than an hour, with little goalmouth excitement and the home side fired up and working relentlessly. Luton looked less fluent than of late, seemingly missing the injured Guttridge in the middle of the park. The breakthrough finally arrived when Elliott headed the hosts in front from close range after Roberts' cross from the right eluded McNulty. It was the first time we'd fallen behind in 1,872 minutes of league football (more than 31 hours), and the first goal conceded in 564 minutes of action, easily beating our previous best.

Within a few minutes, Still had reacted. Three subs were thrown on, but the struggle to create clear openings continued and we looked set to tumble to a first defeat in twenty-seven league games. It would surely not fatally wound our promotion bid, but would be a sickening outcome all the same. Then, with 89 minutes on the clock, salvation came...

McNulty collected the ball on the halfway line and slipped it to McGeehan, who squared it to the feet of Henry. The skipper advanced down the flank, played a simple one-two with Robinson and swung over a swirling cross. The effervescent McGeehan leaped high to nod it down, where Cullen swivelled brilliantly to blast it into the net from close range, a strike remarkably similar to David Platt's 1990 World Cup effort for England against Belgium. Has an away team's goal ever been as loudly and rapturously acclaimed as this? The roar could surely be heard echoing for miles across the Fens. Even Money mentioned the immense reaction in his post-match interview. Town players celebrated wildly in front of the away end. Ecstasy snatched from the jaws of defeat. Fifty seconds after the ball hit the net, another roar went up 42 miles away at Kenilworth Road where the game was being streamed live, with a short time delay, to a packed audience in the Eric Morecambe Suite. The game ended 1-1, and although the draw meant nothing changed at the top of the table, it felt like we'd won promotion in that single moment when Cullen hit the net.

Not just a goal, but '2,000 journeys home rescued,' according to scribe Kevin Crowe, who would later wax lyrical about the finest sight and sound in football being men, women and children singing and pogoing to the final whistle and beyond into the chilly Cambridgeshire night. Although most of us believed the title was already safe before the game, John Still would state that this was the moment he knew for sure we were up and away and into the Football League. For without Cullen's equaliser, Cambridge would have closed the gap a little and had the impetus to have a real go at reeling us back in. But now, fifteen points adrift and Luton still buoyant, their cause was surely a hopeless one. Still, his players and staff, did a slow lap of honour to a thunderous reception from the Luton fans, the manager looking as if he might be close to tears.

He confirmed shortly afterwards,

Emotional? Of course it is, because it's a really weird situation in managing football clubs. I'm here to serve them [the fans], they're not here to serve me, this is their football club, it was their football club long before I came and it will be their football club when I'm gone. I just want to do everything I can to give them back something they thought was taken away unfairly and I know the passion of these people. I've got to know the supporters, know how they think, know how they felt and I just want to do everything I can to give them back something they felt was taken away from them wrongfully. If I can do that I will be very proud. In that last 10 to 15 minutes they raised the volume, never stopped going, never stopped getting behind the team and when I look in the paper tomorrow, if it gives the name of the scorer as Cullen, in brackets it should also say 2,200 supporters.

What a great speech – no wonder we love him! The positive vibes from this unforgettable night continued all week, with the club announcing a few days later it had taken legal steps to protect its image. It had been arranged that Trust in Luton, the official fans' shareholding in the club, would now have the legal right to veto any changes in LTFC's name, kit colours, crest and mascot identity. The idea was to protect against the type of unwanted interference seen recently at Hull City and Cardiff City, where foreign owners wanted to make changes against the fans' wishes. Along with this announcement, Still addressed Luton fans at a special meet-the-manager session at the club, and was clearly still on a high after the late drama at Cambridge.

He revealed he'd been thoroughly professional for 89 minutes and was treating it like any other game until Cullen's goal went in, at which point 'I felt like a little kid!' He added, 'Promotion is the best feeling in the world, it really is, and you are going to feel it!' There were more lumps in throats when a fan stood up and addressed Still directly: 'Thank you for giving me some pride back in being a Luton supporter.' The reaction to this wasn't nearly as loud as the roar at Cambridge two nights earlier, but was no less heartfelt.

Unbeaten in twenty-seven, Luton had eleven games left and the title was almost within grasp. Cambridge needed a miracle to catch up and the calculators were out, and the pubs and internet forums alive with debate over which of the eleven games would be the one at which we clinched our place back in the promised land. Right on cue, as if to warn us against complacency, mid-table Woking came to Kenilworth Road, put in a lively display and inflicted our first league defeat in nearly six months. Played on a Monday evening to suit the BT Sport channel's cameras, the visitors rose to the occasion and in the first-half were quickest to nearly every ball, their passing much more snappy and accurate.

Sat behind one goal among the home fans was England cricket captain Alastair Cooke, a former pupil at Bedford School, but among his mates there was no sign of his Luton-supporting colleague Monty Panesar. In the second period, Luton looked a little more incisive, perhaps due to superior fitness, hitting the post twice and being denied two blatant penalties, notably an incident in which Gray was hauled down. After all the recent publicity about forwards who dive, and about how referees are influenced by big crowds, one suspected the referee erred on the side of caution here. The officials also got it in the neck for ignoring Ruddock being pulled down, an 87th minute incident that led to the only goal of the game, Sole heading home after Murtagh's first effort hit the bar. Sad to see the unbeaten run end, but nobody was panicking yet. One observant fellow pointed out that it was our first defeat of the entire season in which we'd finished with eleven men on the field.

The following Saturday saw a return to business as normal when struggling Chester were the visitors, brushed aside 3-0 to find themselves in distinct danger of relegation. Luton's management drummed up a little bit of extra drama before kick-off, staging a vote among fans over next season's kit, the choice being orange or the traditional white shirts. The result was to be 'announced' by the players emerging from the tunnel wearing the winning colour, we were told. Four thousand took part and, by a tiny majority, orange won the day. And there was further fashion news – this game's huge crowd of 8,475 included 100 Muslim women and girls wearing special headscarves – attending the game as part of an initiative to encourage more people from the local South Asian community to watch live football. Called 'From Headscarves to Football Scarves', the scheme's main aim was to boost social integration in the region.

For more than an hour we were frustrated by hard-working Chester, unable to get our passing together, and a goalless draw looked likely. A few in the crowd seemed to be getting a little nervous following our run of two draws, a defeat and now today's struggle. But such worries were laid firmly to rest in an emphatic final 20 minutes, sub Robinson opening the floodgates when his deep cross swirled unintentionally into the top corner of the net. It was a world-class fluke, but he put the ball into the danger area and got lucky, so we were glad of the break on such a day like today! Gray and Benson banged in further quickfire goals, and we enjoyed a somewhat flattering scoreline of 3-0. The contest featured a nice little 15-minute cameo from new signing Luke Rooney (no relation, although Wayne's brother was on the field, playing for Chester), who arrived only twenty-four hours earlier, a free agent since being released by Swindon a few months ago.

Two tough northern away trips were next on the agenda, to fellow promotion-chasers Grimsby and Halifax. Things started badly for the Tuesday night Luton contingent heading into Blundell Park – radio commentator Simon Pitts was refused entry because he was carrying fish and chips. It was a controversial and unwelcome decision by a steward, which was soon matched by equally baffling calls from the referee, especially after Ruddock was pulled down inside the area and nothing given. Grimsby's Disley had a header cleared off the line before the Mariners' pressure was rewarded, and they took the lead through former Hatter Neilson's 12-yard drive. Luton hit back immediately when the home side failed to clear a Lawless cross, the ball falling for Robinson to crack an equaliser from 10 yards. On the hour mark, Town engineered a counter-attack down the left and Griffiths hammered a low shot against the post, Benson showing brilliant control to force the rebound in. Town were grateful to Tyler for a fine acrobatic late save, which kept the unbeaten away run intact.

A delighted Still commended the youthful midfield of McGeehan, Ruddock and Robinson, all doing a man's job since the loss to injury of the experienced Guttridge and Smith. But the manager was almost lost for words at the giant 'John Still is God' banner that appeared among the travelling faithful: 'Very nice, but I'm really just part of the team,' he said, adding special praise for the 410 who made the difficult journey. 'If I could have done, I would have shaken hands with them all. Kissed the women, but shaken hands with the men. Absolutely fantastic.' We now sat a mind-blowing seventeen points clear at the top, although Cambridge had two games in hand. The fat lady wouldn't be taking the stage to sing for a week or two, but at this rate she may need to get her costume ready and start practising those scales!

Against a Halifax side hungry for a late run into the play-off zone, Luton found themselves under the cosh for long periods. To the disappointment of a splendid away following of 1,179 (a round trip of 350 miles) we fell behind early when a corner was headed firmly home by Roberts amid some suspect marking. Chances for both sides followed, but the Shaymen deservedly clinched the points midway through the second half when Gregory, Gray's main rival for the Confernce Golden Boot, powered through an under-manned defence to stroke home the second. Eleven points from seven games during March didn't match the superlative consistency between December and February, but it was enough to keep things well on track.

April 2014: The Party that Lasted Three Weeks

April – the final push. Would we have the luxury of a gentle jog over the finish line, would it be a late sprint, or maybe an undignified and exhausted stagger? You can never be quite sure at Luton Town, where things are often achieved the hard way.

There were only three more away trips left, the first of which was to relegation-threatened Dartford on a Tuesday evening, a tricky venue that promised lots of lovely traffic congestion and parking issues to overcome. The travelling orange army was nevertheless almost 2,000 strong and easily outnumbered home fans. Among them was Ron Goddard, stationmaster for the the Great Whipsnade Railway (aka *The Jumbo Express*), a narrow gauge heritage railway that operates within Whipsnade Zoo, a couple of miles west of Luton. Ron's job meant he knew all about transport logistics, and his devotion to the Hatters meant he knew all about the trials and tribulations of touring the non-League circuit too. He reported,

> Dartford was always going to be a tough trip, leaving Whipsnade Zoo after a day on the footplate. Hearing about an M1 accident we decided to go via Hatfield and by-pass it, which worked well. If it had not been for a parking nightmare [at Dartford] we would have made kick-off! Once inside the ground our nightmare continued as we struggled to find a place to stand; the railings that encompassed the standing area gave few opportunities to enter. We ended up by a corner flag, but at least Luton were attacking this end. We moved at half-time to be nearer the half-way line, which proved better than wasting time looking for non-existent food. Toilets? No need for many it appears! Quite simply Dartford is the worst ground I have been to in five years – I actually felt unsafe. Thank the Lord we will never have a reason to attend again!

Ron and fellow Luton fans' discomfort increased after 34 minutes of action when Suarez rose high to head home a corner. An ugly challenge on Lawless by Clark saw the Luton man limp away relatively unscathed, but the ref saw it clearly and Clark was red carded. Luton pushed hard for an equaliser but nothing went their way until the closing stages. With less than 10 minutes left, Henry fed Gray, who touched the ball to the onrushing Ruddock, who smashed a fabulous effort high into the net before the 'keeper had a chance to move. Without the netting to stop it, the ball would probably have travelled across half of Kent. The next couple of minutes saw Luton camped in the Dartford half, pressing for a winner, sub Rooney playing a prominent role. After a series of close things, Henry's cross was powered home by the head of Gray. It was victory snatched from the jaws of defeat and the celebrations were massive, Gray losing his shirt and somehow escaping injury when a wild knee-slide went badly wrong. Our tenth away day triumph and the table showed that three wins from the final six games would clinch the title for sure, regardless of Cambridge's results.

Still told the press of his delight at the 'new Luton' that had been blossoming in recent months. Not for the first time he spelled out how other people in football advised him against taking the Luton job because of the unrealistic and intimidating expectation levels, but he was glad he'd accepted the challenge. He said the old chestnut about our crowd turning on their own players had been consigned to history – for nowadays Luton fans actually got louder as games went on, even when we were behind, citing Dartford as a prime example.

Aldershot were in town five days later, a crowd of more than 8,500 packed in, and a couple of smoke bombs were set off by Shots fans. Town looked a little tired and unsettled after a goalless first half, but rarely looked like conceding until near the end, when Tyler had to pull off a truly remarkable save to prevent an own goal. The game's only score arrived with the clock at 4.45 p.m., sub Howells crossing for McGeehan to dive courageously among flailing legs at the near post to head the ball home on 85 minutes. He overcame his grogginess to join in the celebrations, but all the pats on his sore head from teammates proved a little too much and he was soon substituted. Poor Aldershot, labouring to stave off relegation after a points deduction, felt hard done by and were consoled by an ovation from home fans at the end. It left us a healthy thirteen points clear at the top, but as Cambridge still had six games left, promotion couldn't be celebrated quite yet.

The Holy Grail got that little bit closer just three days later, when Tamworth were the visitors. Knowing defeat would condemn them to almost certain relegation, the opposition arrived late due to traffic congestion, only thirteen away fans completing the journey on this Tuesday evening. It meant the 8,554 gate was the best turnout of Luton fans for a single game in several years (excluding the JPT and play-off finals). Luton's task now was simply to get their nose across that finish line, and much of this contest proved a rather scrappy affair, although we did step things up after the interval with sub Lawless looking outstanding. An unwelcome sight was twenty-seven-goal Gray departing early with a knee problem. McGeehan tapped in Howells' pinpoint cross to settle any anxieties, and Cullen pounced to net Lawless' perfectly weighted pass to make it a routine 2-0 win.

The big moment was getting very close. Luton would be crowned champions if Cambridge were to lose their Thursday night game at Woking, but the champagne went back in the fridge when Money's men cruised to a 3-0 win. We now knew victory at home to Braintree in a Saturday lunchtime kick-off would do the job. It was in our own hands and the promotion party could be on our own ground – just what everybody wanted. Naturally, the game proved a 10,000 sell-out and it boiled up into one hell of a week. Luton Town were making headlines via news outlets that had forgotten we existed, and long-suffering fans who never went away were spilling out their emotional stories all over the place.

The Independent zoomed in on chairman Nick Owen, who told them, 'I've seen sixteen promotions and relegations, and in many ways this one means the most because it comes after such a long time of decline and pain.'

Hampshire-based fan Nick Pirie, writing for the Luton Town America website, summarised this remarkable season in a way that resonated with many of us 6,000 bruised but buoyant regulars:

A new manager, again, told us it would take time. The fact we weren't troubling the play-offs a year ago meant we had time to adjust to this idea. We weren't even dreaming of automatic promotion. Defeat, lucky late draw, defeat. Well, he did tell us it was a long term project. Then the run started. We were picking up points without looking convincing, but something happened. The crowd suddenly started to back the team. The team responded to the crowd, or did the crowd respond to the team? Suddenly we did look a team. That huge gap Cambridge had created started to narrow. We started to look at top spot. Cambridge started to wobble. And now we are standing on the brink. It's not confirmed yet ... but we will be up as champions. How good will that 'C' look next to our name? We're on our way back. It's been a long time coming but there's a new dawn breaking.

Braintree at home on Saturday 12 April was built up into a real carnival day. The day the dream would finally become reality. Braintree were a well-organised, feisty little team, so it would have been nice to have had easier opposition, but who cared? Nothing could go wrong now surely? Some extra capacity was found from somewhere, 10,020 were squeezed into the ground, the biggest crowd for seven years. Due to the demands of live television and a 7-minute delay in tribute to Hillsborough victims, the game would kick-off at 12.52 p.m., we were told. Luton fans would have been up and about early anyway today, preparing for celebrations that could explode into life around 2.30 p.m. The town centre and the LU4 district occupied by the old stadium were buzzing all morning.

Excitement spilled over long before a ball was kicked. On BBC local radio one over-exuberant presenter even called Luton 'the home of football'. People headed for the ground early, with a new spring in their step. Orange-clad fans strolled past the site of the Bedfordshire Yeoman pub, now a building materials sales yard, but a popular fans watering hole last time we played a League match. The halal fish and chip shop on the corner of Clifton Road was doing brisk business – apparently many folk reckoned a dose of fried food with batter was just what they needed to ease stomachs queasy with nerves. Two coaches from Essex were parked in Oak Road, but all was quiet at the away fans turnstiles – the ninety-four travellers were apparently already inside and no more were coming. On social media, the messages cascaded from across the globe – in Adelaide, for example, somebody was more worried about Luton Town than an impending cyclone threatening that city!

People told their Facebook and Twitter pals they were 'really buzzing today'. Behind the Kenilworth Road stand people milled about in the sunshine, many smoking nervously. One local woman was dressed in full Viking regalia. Nobody seemed particularly curious as to why. Inside the ground a great atmosphere was building long before kick-off, and on the pitch a television crew interviewed David Pleat and ex-England 'keeper David James. The latter had recently been helping with coaching at Luton as he worked towards his FA and UEFA badges. Among the banners was a big Greek national flag bearing the legend 'Luton Town Kefalonika'. It felt a lot like the days of old, which was presumably why some fans wheeled out the old songs: 'Olé, olé olé olé' and 'Hark now hear the Luton sing' and similar uplifting nonsense.

An announcement about the twenty-fifth anniversary of the Hillsborough tragedy saw the players line up around the centre circle and the crowd noise drop to an impeccable silence. After a short while, the referee's whistle blew, most fans naturally assuming this was the signal to end the period of silence. A huge cheer went up, but the ref was actually signalling the start not the end, and nobody on the field moved. After a moment's confusion and realisation that complete silence wouldn't be achieved again, the fans came up with a fine bit of improvisation and started applauding in tribute to the ninety-six fallen instead.

The match got underway and the carnival atmosphere was rather spoiled when it became clear Braintree hadn't read the script. Incredibly, Luton fell 0-3 behind. This was party-pooping to an extreme degree. Was it the curse of the live television cameras striking us again? At 0-2 we had a great chance to get back into the game, but Braintree's 'keeper brought down Benson to prevent him scoring into an empty net. The custodian was sent off and Luton got a free-kick outside the area, which came to nothing. With their sub 'keeper in place, the only change was in Braintree's formation, which went from 4-4-2 to 4-4-1, and saw them continue to scrap ferociously. Luton were badly missing leading scorer Gray, plus Lawless, who went off injured early, and, more than ever, the guile of Guttridge. For an hour we looked tense and subdued. But after falling 0-3 behind, we finally launched a fightback and the deflated atmosphere improved. A penalty from Howells after a disputed handball, and then a powerful deflected shot by Wall brought it back to 2-3.

Now it was most definitely game on again. We could still settle this today. Noise levels were sky-high as we hit the woodwork twice, and McNulty and Cullen missed decent chances. But a third goal proved just out of reach as we ran out of time. This was not to be the day. Gritty Braintree had now beaten us in four out of six meetings in the Conference, a great achievement for a small club that was not even fully professional. They now had the mantle previously held by York as our bogey side. Their hardy ninety-four fans started singing 'We're just a pub team from Essex', which was either modesty or irony, hard to tell, and seemed to be the only song they knew. Although their fixture pile-up had led to a couple of defeats last week, they'd bounced back in style today and still had an outside chance of the play-offs. Manager Alan Devonshire had undergone quite a transformation over the years, a slim, skilful will-o'-the-wisp in his prime for West Ham and England, he was now flat-capped, rotund, clean shaven on the upper lip and apparently a preacher of solid, stodgy football. He also stood accused of being ungracious in post-match interviews, for despite this day's win he rambled on about Luton being favoured by the officials.

The 2-3 scoreline represented a huge anti-climax for Luton, but the ten-point lead we still maintained at the end of the weekend was ample consolation. Just think how bad this day would have felt had we still been neck and neck with Cambridge? Perhaps the biggest let-down of all was the strong likelihood the title would not now be clinched in front of the Luton faithful at Kenilworth Road. Our next home game was nine days away, by which time it would surely be sorted out, quite possibly by Cambridge dropping a point or two. It was now a case of preparing ourselves for a night beside the radio, or in front of a computer screen to await our fate. On Tuesday 15 April, Luton had no game, but Cambridge had a tough fixture at the home of play-off rivals Kidderminster. If the Us lost, it would be all over and Luton champions. A draw or a win for Money's men would mean the wait going on.

As you will know, dear reader, if you were paying attention at the beginning of this book, Kidderminster won 2-0, meaning Luton were now mathematically uncatchable at the top. The title was ours. It was all over bar the shouting (and the drinking, the partying and all the other forms of making merry). There was one hell of an explosion of joy and relief that night – as detailed in my introductory chapter – and the party would last a good three weeks or so. With three matches still to play in the Conference, we could call ourselves a Football League club again, some 1,810 days having passed since we said farewell at Brentford's Griffin Park in May 2009.

Players, management and fans could all bask in the glow of success at long last. The end of an era was nigh and blogger David Mosque felt it was a good time to recognise the achievement of the club's board in the past five years:

It has been a horrible, messy, uncomfortable and occasionally fun ride. The board have learned so many lessons. As we tumbled out of the League they were learning about how to run a football club from scratch amid crisis after crisis. They inherited a juggernaut, careering out of control downhill, plummeting through the divisions at top speed. They learned on the job, made mistakes, but in appointing John Still made the soundest decision for many a long year at this club. Five long seasons of our history had to be endured in non-League before we could get back to where we belong. But you have to prune a rosebush back to allow it to flourish. Consider ourselves pruned. Consider ourselves flourishing. The turning point this year? As plain as your nose on the face it was the 3-2 win over Lincoln where that fan let his thoughts be known at half-time, and Ronnie Henry let his be known at full time. Within a week the fan was at the training ground and then in the huddle, and by the next home game we were all on board.

And so the penultimate away trip of the entire non-League era was to be a sunny Saturday out to the London borough of Bexley for another lunchtime kick-off. Was this the most 'village green-ish' of all our Conference trips? Quite possibly. We were greeted at Welling United's Park View Road ground by A4 sheets of paper stuck on posts, some congratulating us on winning the title, others bearing today's team line-ups. Quaint, but much appreciated. There was a friendly atmosphere here that made it feel rather like a Saturday afternoon church fete; there was a young lad commentating on events over the PA – presumably for the benefit of those who couldn't quite see – including pre-match presentation ceremonies in front of the tiny main stand. It was the Wings' golden jubilee year, so they were entitled to have fun and enjoy a day when the champions were in town.

Leafy Danson Park is adjacent to one end of the stadium, and it proved a good venue for watching the world go by outside if the football got a bit dull. You could also get a good view of the action inside if you went past on a red London bus. At one point, a group of strollers in Danson Park ambled over and peered over the fence to see what the fuss was all about. Once the game was underway, we all had a good chortle when a fierce effort on goal by Wall cleared the Welling crossbar, and everything else too, sailing out across the main A207 road and into the forecourt of a Fiat garage. The ball bounced around crazily among the Puntos and the Pandas.

Cullen livened things up on the field, coolly converting a pass from Gray to put us ahead. The PA announcer then proclaimed the arrival of a first-half Welling substitution, and took the opportunity to add, 'Could the Luton fan behind the Supreme Engraving advertising board return that match ball please?' Unlucky chap, busted in a very public way.

There was little else of note before half-time, although gasps of astonishment greeted the moment a steward suddenly marched from one corner flag to the other, choosing a route right through the goalmouth while play was still going on. Perhaps the pathway behind the goal was too narrow for him, or perhaps he feared the packed terrace of Luton fans were the types who didn't use deodorant? Halfway through the second half, Gray snatched a typical goal, latching on to a long pass and powering ahead of his marker to thrash a shot home. Lafayette curled a shot home for the home side with 10 minutes left, but it was merely a consolation before the final whistle signalled a mass pitch invasion by celebrating Lutonians.

John Still and the players attempted their usual post-match huddle, but it became a very public event when they were joined on the field by a large proportion of their 2,000 supporters. It then became a lap of honour, Still amiably strolling the perimeter of the pitch like a pied piper, shaking hands, giving high fives when requested, and posing for selfies with countless admirers. The players did the same and the whole mob ended up in or near the main stand, singing, dancing, taking each other's picture and generally enjoying the warm glow of success. Incidentally, the day's crowd figures produced the latest oddity in this season-full of bizarre stats: a massive 75 per cent of the 2,650 were away supporters. Surely some sort of record?

With Easter Sunday to recover from the Welling party and its aftermath, the next, and bigger celebrations would be at the Bank Holiday Monday's contest at Kenilworth Road against Forest Green, after which the Skrill Premier Trophy and medals would be handed over. Easter periods in the past have often been bad news for Luton Town, promotion chances fluffed or relegations sealed, but this time we could devour our chocolate eggs with big foolish grins on our faces. On the Monday morning, the party clothes were coming out and fans like Karen Samm were in a real quandary. She posted a picture on Facebook of her washing line filled with Luton shirts and T-shirts of all description and vintage, and asked plaintively: 'Oh what is a girl to wear? Decisions, decisions!'

By lunchtime, town centre pubs were reportedly full to bursting with orange-shirted hordes. Close to the ground, at the top of Hazelbury Crescent and looking down the hill, it was almost reminiscent of Empire Way at Wembley with all the hats and flags advancing up the slope to the ground. There was the pungent odour of hot dogs, the sound of klaxon horns, and a real cup final atmosphere. There were even pirate souvenir sellers with all sorts of tat on offer. They had hats shaped like traffic cones – presumably deemed appropriate purely because they happened to be orange. The biggest home crowd rolled up since Sunderland were here in 2007 (10,042), for nobody could bear to miss this party, not even the wife of local newspaperman Mark Wood, who was nine months pregnant and might have given birth at any minute. Her mother had also made it over from New York, so would no doubt keep an eye on her.

Forest Green were short-staffed and unable to name a full set of subs and had recalled the loaned-out Jason Walker to play against his former club.

The man never forgiven for messing up in Luton's 2011 Manchester penalty shoot-out was booed whenever he got the ball, but, sensibly, didn't respond. However, when he was eventually subbed, he chose to ignore the dugouts and headed the opposite way, straight down the tunnel. Curious.

Today, the champions were also without one or two key men, and we fell behind on 34 minutes when McNulty handled and Klukowski netted from the spot. But on the stroke of half-time, Russell brought down Gray, who levelled from the spot for his twenty-ninth goal of the season, having been given special dispensation to take the kick to help his bid for a thirty-goal haul. McGeehan forced the ball home after his own 20-yard shot was only half saved and then hard-working Cullen crossed for Gray to head in and reach that milestone he'd desperately sought. Gray was taken off after this, apparently to protect a minor injury, a move that appeared to annoy somebody in an executive box behind the dugout. Something untoward was said, and Still uncharacteristically reacted to this, hurling a bottle of water to the floor and indulging in a bout of finger-wagging admonishment. It seemed out of character in the circumstances, but perhaps the boss had overheated in the splendid orange shirt and dark suit he was wearing in the sunshine? Any bad feeling didn't linger, though, and Cullen, desperate to get into double figures for the season, conjured up a brilliant solo goal in the last minute – an effort that bore comparison to the well-remembered Paul Walsh effort at the same end back in 1982 against Notts County. Forest Green attempted to play good football and perhaps the 4-1 scoreline flattered Luton a little, but you couldn't argue with such confident and decisive finishing.

The presentations were able to go ahead on the field, despite a premature and light-hearted pitch invasion that was quickly dispersed without problems. The players were introduced one-by-one to come forward for their medals, some of them carrying their children in the strange, recently established tradition for these occasions. I believe it was Dennis Wise and his toddler who started it all when Chelsea won the FA Cup? The honour of bringing the trophy to the pitch was bestowed on John Buttle, a real Luton stalwart who had worked here behind the scenes for many years. There was ticker tape and champagne to spray around and subsequently the inevitable full-scale pitch invasion. The squad and management headed into the main stand to look out on an amazing sea of orange before them. Appropriate songs blasted from the PA system, including, of course, Eric and Ernie's 'Bring me Sunshine'.

There were speeches from the manager, the managing director and the skipper, and a spot of rapping from hip-hop specialist Robinson. McGeehan, who must have posed for a thousand selfies, somehow got hold of mascot Happy Harry's detachable giant head during all this, threw it up in the air and then looked on in horror as it sailed unintentionally out above the crowd and came crashing down, fortunately not injuring anybody. It was okay, Mac, we saw it coming and ducked! It was later reported the player lost his medal during this episode, but was later reunited with it.

McGeehan, on loan from relegation-haunted Norwich, was loving his time in the limelight, particularly when the fans sang for him to stay at Luton, and after the mascot dismembering he threw his boots to the eager crowd. Other players liked this idea and followed suit, but Pelly Ruddock clearly cherished his footwear and didn't look so keen. He had to be held down by teammates who prised them off his feet, Gray sending one flying out into the crowd, and accidentally flinging the other into the roof of the stand where it got lodged. It could be there for years, or at least until we got a new ground, suggested one fan. The club later published a photo showing it had been rescued by an employee clearly unafraid of heights.

The third goal against Forest Green had taken us to the 100-goal mark, and now a win in the final match at Hyde would take the points tally past the century to 101. What a contrast the day at Hyde would provide to the tears and heartache suffered on our previous visit to the Manchester area on the final day of a season. More than 2,250 made the long trip for a 5.30 p.m. kick-off, many in fancy dress – the Blues Brothers, the Super Mario Brothers, chickens and Fred Flintstone were all spotted at various points along the M1 and M6. The announcer at Ewen Fields wished Luton good luck in the Football League next season, and there was a raucous welcome for the team from a crowd that was more than 80 per cent Luton fans. What a difference a season makes – only one player started today (goalkeeper Tyler) who had also started the game at Hyde the previous season. There were various records to be broken or established by Luton on this day, but humble Hyde were more anxious to merely avoid being humiliated, for they sat bottom of the table with just ten points from forty-five games, and hadn't won a single home match all season.

There was a guard of honour from red-shirted Hyde as the Hatters emerged, lining up in the centre circle for a special wave and acknowledgement to the fans for the amazing support since August. Apart from one tower block of apartments nearby, it was a bucolic scene with trees behind the Luton fans on all four sides of the Walker Lane ground. When finally underway, the last of our 230-plus games of the non-League era was, perhaps unsurprisingly, not a classic.

A Hyde shot struck the top of Tyler's crossbar and the home side looked far livelier than their record indicated. We waited much longer than expected for a Luton goal, Wall doing the honours by galloping clear of the home defence to slide the ball home 20 minutes from time. Some fans from behind the goal invaded the pitch to envelop Wall and McGeehan, one snatching the ball and lashing it into the net, but it was all light-hearted stuff and they soon retreated. Near the end, radio listeners were told that Lee Gregory was not being used by Halifax in their simultaneous game, meaning Andre Gray had definitely won the coveted Golden Boot award, whether or not he scored today. There was to be one more notable occurrence before the last of the final whistles sounded. With the clock showing 89 minutes and 47 seconds, Still sent on Jonathan Smith as a substitute, four months to the day after he had had his leg cruelly broken at Barnet. The reception Smudger got was astonishing, the player admitting later he was quite overwhelmed by the sheer scale of it. Who said there was no room for sentiment in modern football?

Mr Backhouse then sounded the final whistle to bring a momentous season to a close. Luton fans swept onto the pitch itching to get their third successive post-match party underway. After the five years of grief and disappointment, there was an awful lot of steam being let off just now, and no wonder. We Luton fans had learned to make the most of the good times, because there were always plenty of lows in between. One of the travellers, referring to himself as 'Woodsyhatter', enjoyed his day at Hyde but hoped never to go back:

> We had the Blues Brothers chain-smoking around us and passing cans of beer around, four funky chickens and a very large monkey, and I can assure you I wasn't the one on the funny fags! Oh, how we'll miss these non-League grounds – not! The two portaloos at each corner of the ground kept saying to me, 'Please Luton, never again'. We did our bit at the end by trying to flatten the bobbles out of the pitch by running across it. And I never thought I'd hear myself saying 'Bring on Accrington Stanley!'

May 2014: 'All of a Sudden the Sun's Come Out'

The relief and unbridled joy at finally returning to the League may have first exploded in mid-April, but three weeks later it was showing no signs of abating. Various dinners, presentations and other ceremonies remained, notably a parade in Luton town centre and civic reception at the town hall. Luton Borough Council joined the fun by having the town hall steps painted bright orange in readiness.

Back in 1919, the citizens of Luton stormed their town hall and burned it down during a riot sparked by unhappy ex-servicemen. Ninety-five years later, the atmosphere was far more convivial as an estimated 12,000 people descended on the St George's Square area on a Sunday lunchtime to laud their Hatters heroes. The scale of the day's events and sheer size of the turnout must surely be unprecedented in non-League history. It compared well to the scenes in 1988 and 2005, when the League Cup and League One trophies were paraded here. Returning from oblivion was clearly important enough to stand alongside those very special days.

Fans gathered early for the best vantage points, some congregating near the football ground to see the open-topped bus set off, some lining the route, but the vast majority filling the town centre. Here the players left their big, red bus to mount a huge temporary stage before gathering on the town hall steps and then up on the balcony. Early on, with the empty bus awaiting arrival of the players in Maple Road, a lone yellow-shirted Watford fan strolled by, suddenly plucking up the courage to wave his arms and shout about his team before exiting hastily stage right. The Luton fans crowded around the bus were not interested in rising to the bait and ignored him. Eventually, the parade wound up at St George's Square, speeches were made and at one point the fan who had the infamous public spat with Ronnie Henry was spotted in the massive audience and hauled up on stage to say a few words.

After several years of indifference and minimal coverage, the media were very interested in Luton Town again. John Still told all and sundry about the new unified club and the importance of his 'team' ethic, but was honest enough to admit success had come along earlier than he'd foreseen. Although he'd taken two other clubs from Conference to Football League, this had been his most remarkable year, he said. Speaking to Talksport radio, he revealed the first man to congratulate him had been Brendan Rogers, manager of Premiership title-chasers Liverpool. Asked for his favourite moment from a season of countless highlights, Still went for the late equaliser at Cambridge ('We knew then it would be so hard for others to catch us') and of the many records created, his favourite was the nineteen-point margin by which the league was won ('A staggering achievement considering we lost key players to injury').

Still's genial and open manner in interviews was undoubtedly one of the reasons he had become popular at Luton, and fans were quick to call Talksport to pay tribute while Still was on the air. An example was Aussie fan Billy, who said,

> This man has given us our club back. I came over from Australia for one game and they beat Hereford 7-0. The Ruddock goal that day would have graced the Premiership. Fantastic. I have mates all over the globe and we'd virtually stopped talking about Luton on social media and via email, but now we're all doing that again.

While Cambridge won their way back to the League via the play-offs during May, a stress-free Still and his men were in demand at all manner of functions and dinners, one of which saw Still given a Lifetime Achievement

Award by the *Non-League Paper*. And as the events of 2013/14 began to sink in properly, he could reflect on what had happened:

> The enormity of what has gone on at Luton is unbelievable. I feel that for all those people that felt this club was wronged, I've helped right that wrong. That gives me a very, very special feeling and it's probably as big as anything I've ever done professionally. What we've done here is recreate this club. I did feel there was resentment when I came, I felt an anger, a malaise. Now I feel I've been part of a group of people that have reinvented this club.

The media attention focused on Luton even spread to the celebrity world. When superstar David Bowie screened a message to a music industry awards night, he talked about his record company boss Rob Stringer, a vice-president of the Hatters and devoted fan. Bowie said, 'When Rob asked me if I minded if he took a few Saturdays off from his duties in order to catch the Luton Town FC fixtures, how could I refuse? It's the least I could offer to the man who with his own hands pulled my album to number one throughout the world!'

Less than ten years ago, Luton were playing clubs like West Ham, WBA, Stoke, Hull, Sunderland, Southampton and Crystal Palace on a weekly basis. All of a sudden, we were sentenced to a five-year stretch facing the likes of Alfreton, Braintree, Ebbsfleet and Welling. But the hard-core support never wavered, they came back week after week in great numbers, however depressing things became. This club simply refused to sink permanently into oblivion. Although he certainly didn't do it alone, the man who made all the difference and turned things around was a sixty-two-year-old former salesman from the East End called John Leonard Still.

Luton Town were back where they belonged, and as Still said, 'I'm proud to have given those fans their dignity back. All of a sudden the sun's come out.'

Appendix

(Statistics here refer to Conference and play-off matches only, not cup competitions)

Conference era stats, August 2009–April 2014:

236 games, 122 wins, 65 draws, 49 losses, 428 scored, 223 conceded
Biggest win: 8-0 (*v.* Hayes & Yeading, March 2010)
Biggest loss: 1-5 (*v.* Gateshead, April 2013)

Conference era managerial records:

Mick Harford: 12 games (W6-D3-L3)
Alan Nielson (caretaker): 9 games (4-2-3)
Richard Money: 66 games (37-15-14)
Gary Brabin: 52 games (23-20-9)
Paul Buckle: 37 games (18-7-12)
John Still: 61 games (35-18-8)

Achievements in season 2013/14:

- Won Conference by record 19-point margin
- Club record haul of 102 goals
- Club record haul of 101 points
- Club record of 23 clean sheets
- Club record run of 27 games unbeaten
- Club record run of 25 away games unbeaten
- Average attendance: 7,387 (higher than 39 of 92 League clubs)
- Average away fan turnout for Luton trips: 1,086

- Highest Conference scoring rate (average 2.22 per game)
- Best Conference defensive record (average 0.76 conceded per game)
- Biggest away wins in Conference (5-0 at Nuneaton and Alfreton)
- Highest attendance at any Conference match: 10,044 *v.* Forest Green
- Twelve Conference clubs had highest gate of season against Luton
- Best goal difference (+67) in the top five English divisions
- Joint top scorers (102) in the top five English divisions
- Joint second best defence (35) in top five English divisions
- Gained enough points (83) to win Conference title with eight games left
- Conference Golden Boot winner: Andre Gray (30 goals)
- *Non-League Paper* NGA Player of the Year: Steve McNulty
- *Non-League Paper* NGA Young Player of the Year: Andre Gray
- *Non-League Paper* NGA Goalkeeper of the Year: Mark Tyler
- *Non-League Paper* NGA Lifetime Achievement Award: John Still